Vernon L. Kellogg

Common Injurious Insects of Kansas

Vernon L. Kellogg

Common Injurious Insects of Kansas

ISBN/EAN: 9783743323162

Manufactured in Europe, USA, Canada, Australia, Japa

Cover: Foto ©ninafisch / pixelio.de

Manufactured and distributed by brebook publishing software (www.brebook.com)

Vernon L. Kellogg

Common Injurious Insects of Kansas

THE UNIVERSITY OF KANSAS,

LAWRENCE.

DEPARTMENT OF ENTOMOLOGY.

F. H. Snow, Ph. D.
V. L. Kellogg, M. S.

COMMON INJURIOUS INSECTS

OF KANSAS.

BY
VERNON L. KELLOGG.

THE UNIVERSITY.
1892.

PRESS OF HAMILTON PRINTING COMPANY:
EDWIN H. SNOW, STATE PRINTER.

TOPEKA.

PREFATORY NOTE.

The fact that Kansas is annually sustaining a large financial loss because of the attacks of injurious insects on its cereal, garden and fruit crops, a considerable part of which loss is needlessly suffered, is excuse for this pamphlet. Only the commoner, or more important, insect pests working within the State are considered. Nor are all the important pests included; though, of cereal pests, I believe most, if not all, are included.

In compiling the information presented herewith, the writings of reputable economic entomologists, generally, have been consulted and relied on. Bruner of Nebraska, Comstock of New York, Forbes of Illinois, Lintner of New York, Osborn of Iowa, Riley of the United States Agricultural Department, Saunders of Canada, Smith of New Jersey, Weed of New Hampshire, and others, are such entomologists. The Kansas notes have been derived from the reports of the State Board of Agriculture and the State Horticultural Society; from the published notes of Prof. F. H. Snow, of the University of Kansas, Prof. E. A. Popenoe, of the State Agricultural College, and Mr. G. C. Brackett, secretary of the State Horticultural Society; and from the unpublished notes of the Department of Entomology in the University. For valuable suggestions constantly offered during the course of compilation, I am indebted to Chancellor F. H. Snow and Dr. S. W. Williston, of the University.

VERNON L. KELLOGG.

UNIVERSITY OF KANSAS, November 14, 1892.

ACKNOWLEDGMENTS.

My thanks are due Mr. G. C. Brackett, secretary of the Kansas State Horticultural Society, who most kindly put at my disposal electrotypes of figures 4, 37, 38, 39, 40, 41, 42, 43, 44, 46 (4), 48, 49, 50, 52, 54. All of these figures are original with Dr. C. V. Riley.

The electrotype of figure 45 was loaned by Prof. E. A. Popenoe, of the State Agricultural College, Manhattan.

The plate so fully illustrating the life-history of the Hessian Fly, figure 16, the various parts original with Riley, Burgess, and Packard, was loaned by Hon. M. Mohler, secretary of the State Board of Agriculture.

The plates for all the other figures (excepting figures 1 and 13, both after Riley) were made expressly for this volume by A. Zeese & Co., of Chicago, from original drawings, and from reduced, rearranged or otherwise altered copies of existing plates, as follows: Figures 2, 3, 5, 7, e of 12, a of 14, a, c of 17, a of 19, 20, 21, 22, 23, b, d, e, f, g, h of 24, a of 25, c, d, e of 27, 28 (2), b, d of 29, a of 30, a of 31, a of 32, a of 33, c, d of 34, 35 (3), 53, a of 55, 56 (5), b, c of 57, 59, a of 60, and a, b, c of 61, are from original drawings made by Miss Mary Wellman, under direction. Figure 6 is a copy of figures selected from plate I (J. H. Emerton), First Annual Report of the U. S. Entomological Commission, 1878; figure 8 is a copy of figures from plate v, Thirteenth Report of the Illinois State Entomologist (Prof. S. A. Forbes); figure 9 is after H. A. Garman; figures 10 and 11 are copies (reduced and rearranged) in outline of the colored figures of plates A and B, Seventeenth Report of the State Entomologist of Illinois (Prof. S. A. Forbes); a, b, c, d of figure 12 are figure 6; b and c of figure 14, e and f of 15, figure 18, and b of 19, are after Riley; c and d of figure 15 are after Glover; b and d of figure 17 are after Forbes; a and c of figure 24 are after H. E. Weed; b and c of figure 25 are after Curtis; figure 26 is after a cut in the *American Naturalist* (*Tyroglyphus sacchari*); a and b of figure 27, c of figure 29, b of figure 31, b of figure 32, b of figure 33, are after Riley; b of figure 30 is after Scudder; a and b of figure 34 are after Popenoe; a of figure 36 is after Riley, and b is after Weed; figure 47 is a rearranged copy of portions of a figure original with Riley; figure 51 is after Packard and Saunders; b of figure 55 is after Popenoe; a of figure 57 is after Riley; figure 58 is after Claparéde; b and c of figure 60 are after Riley.

TABLE OF CONTENTS.

	PAGE.
INTRODUCTION,	1
REMEDIES,	7
Spraying and Dusting,	10
Prevention,	12
INSECTS ATTACKING CEREAL CROPS:	
Corn Insects:	
Chinch-bug,	13
Western Corn-root Worm,	17
Southern Corn-root Worm,	19
Corn-root Louse,	20
Corn-louse,	21
Rocky Mountain Locust,	22
Garden Web-worm,	25
Corn Worm,	27
Other Insects Attacking Corn,	28
Wheat Insects:	
Hessian Fly,	29
Wheat-straw Worm,	35
Wheat-head Army-worm,	37
Fall Army-worm,	39
Other Insects Attacking Wheat,	40
INSECTS ATTACKING OTHER CEREALS AND GRASSES:	
Injurious Grasshoppers:	
Red-legged Locust,	41
Differential Locust,	42
Two-striped Locust,	42
Long-winged Locust,	43
Other Insects Attacking Cereals and Grasses,	49
STORED-GRAIN INSECTS:	
Angoumois Grain Moth,	50
Grain Weevils,	52
Flax-seed Mite,	53
INSECTS ATTACKING GARDEN VEGETABLES:	
Tortoise Beetles,	55
Squash Bug,	56

INSECTS ATTACKING GARDEN VEGETABLES—*Concluded:*
 Harlequin Cabbage Bug, ... 57
 Imported Cabbage-worm, ... 59
 Southern Cabbage-worm, ... 60
 Cabbage Plusia, ... 61
 Pea Weevil, ... 62
 Bean Weevil, ... 63
 Tomato-worm, ... 64
 Cucumber Beetle, ... 65
 Other Insects Attacking Garden Crops, . 66

INSECTS ATTACKING LARGE FRUITS:
 Round-headed Apple-tree Borer, . . 67
 Flat-headed Apple-tree Borer, . 69
 Apple-root Louse, . . . 73
 Spring Canker-worm, 75
 Codlin Moth, . . 78
 Tarnished Plant-bug, . 80
 Apple-tree Twig Borer, . . 81
 Fall Web-worm, ... 83
 Apple-tree Tent Caterpillar, 85
 Plum Curculio, . 87
 Plum Gouger, ... 89
 Cherry Aphis, ... 90
 Peach-tree Borer, ... 91
 Other Insects Attacking Large Fruits, 92

INSECTS ATTACKING SMALL FRUITS:
 Raspberry Slug, ... 93
 Strawberry Leaf-roller, ... 94
 Other Insects Attacking Small Fruits, 95

INSECTS ATTACKING SHADE-TREES:
 White-marked Tussock Moth, 96
 Walnut Moth, . . . 98
 Box-elder Bug, ... 99
 Green-striped Maple-worm, . . . 101
 Bag-worm, ... 103
 Other Insects Attacking Shade-trees, . 105

INSECTS ATTACKING FLOWERS:
 Red Spider, ... 106
 Rose Slug, ... 106

NOXIOUS INSECTS OF THE HOUSEHOLD:
 Cockroaches, ... 108
 Buffalo Beetle, ... 109
 Clothes-moth, ... 110
 Ants, ... 112

APPENDIX:
 The Horn Fly of Cattle, . . 113

ILLUSTRATIONS.

	PAGE.
Angoumois Grain Moth	50
Apple-root Louse	74
Apple-tree Tent Caterpillar	85
Apple-twig Borer	82
Bag-worm	104
Bean Weevil	63
Beetle (biting)	1
Box-elder Bug	100
Buffalo Beetle	109
Cabbage Plusia	61
Chinch-bug	13
Clothes-moth	111
Cockroach	108
Codlin Moth	78
Corn-root Louse	20
Corn-louse	21
Corn Worm	27
Cucumber Beetle	66
Differential Locust	42, 45
Fall Army-worm	39
Fall Web-worm	4, 84
Flat-headed Apple-tree Borer	70
Flax-seed Mite	53
Garden Web-worm	25
Grain Weevil	52
Green-striped Maple-worm	101
Harlequin Cabbage Bug	58
Hessian Fly	30
Imported Cabbage-worm	59
Long-winged Locust	43
Maple Worm	4
Pea Weevil	62
Peach-tree Borer	91
Plum Curculio	87
Plum Gouger	89
Raspberry Slug	93
Red Spider	106
Rocky Mountain Locust	5, 23, 24
Round-headed Apple-tree Borer	67, 68
Southern Cabbage-worm	61
Southern Corn-root Worm	19
Spring Canker-worm	76
Squash Bug	2, 57
Strawberry Leaf-roller	94
Tarnished Plant-bug	80
Tomato-worm	2, 83

Tortoise Beetles 55
Two-striped Locust. 44, 45
Western Corn-root Worm 17
Wheat-head Army-worm 38
Wheat-straw Worm.. 35
White-marked Tussock Moth 96
Yellow-necked Apple-tree Caterpillar 98

NOTE.—The straight line by the side of an insect illustration indicates the natural size of the insect; where this line is wanting, and it is not otherwise stated to be enlarged, the cut is of the natural size of the insect.

INTRODUCTION.

The knowledge of entomology desired by farmers is, as a rule, limited by the actual demands of profitable farming. A knowledge of the life-histories of the Chinch-bug and Hessian Fly is certainly a necessary requisite of the most profitable farming in Kansas; one might even say of any profitable farming. The fruit-grower should know something about borers and Codlin Moths as well as about grafting. But more than this necessary entomological knowledge — and this knowledge is all gathered about the practical application of it, the how and why of remedies — is not being loudly called for by the grain- and vegetable- and fruit-growers. Hence entomological text-books are not crowding everything else off the parlor tables in the farm homes; and a bug is a bug and not much else, to the worker in the fields. It is a fact, however, that the men who do pay some attention to the bugs are helping themselves. For the intelligent application of insecticides (insect-killing substances), some little should be known of the general economy of insect life, and that little may be briefly told.

Broadly speaking, insects may be divided into two great groups, namely, biting insects and sucking insects. The biting insects have jaws, or mandibles, moving laterally, instead of vertically as with us, and fitted for tearing off and masticating foliage, fruits, bark, and even hard wood. They take into their mouths and swallow the succulent tissues of the plant leaf or the dry, tough fibers of woody tissue. They take "solid food." The beetles and the grasshoppers are insects possessing typical biting mouth-parts. The sucking insects, on the

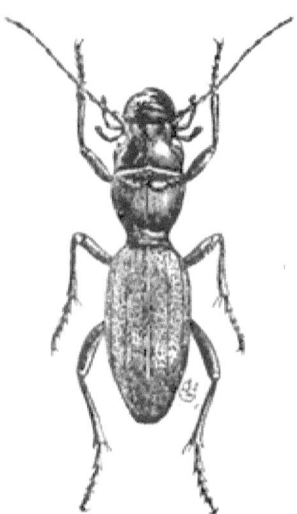

FIG. 1. A BEETLE, with biting mouth-parts.

other hand, have the mouth-parts more or less completely combined into a hollow, pointed beak, which may be thrust through protecting outer envelopes to get at the juices of plants and even animals. The sucking insects live on liquid food. The true bugs, including such well-known forms as the Chinch-bug, Squash-bug, and the plant-lice, are insects possessing typical sucking beaks.

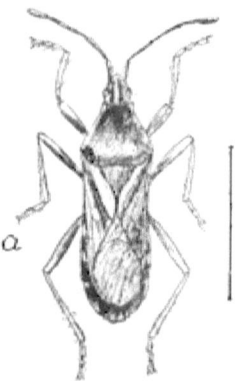

FIG. 2. SQUASH-BUG, with sucking mouth-parts.

This broad distinction between biting and sucking insects is an attractive one, but, unfortunately for its immediate use as a basis for generalizations concerning practical work, complications arise because of the wonderful character of the growth of certain insects. While the young of the Chinch-bug much resemble the parent, having a true sucking beak, and lacking only the wings which are present in the adult, the young of the butterfly or of the moth do not at all resemble the parent forms, and, correlated with the difference in resemblance, have wholly different habits. The adult Tomato-worm Moth, for example, has a

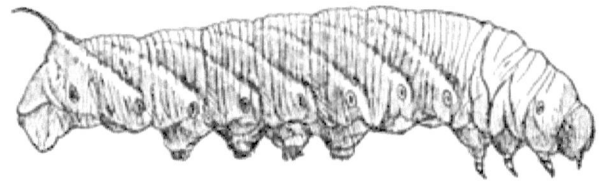

FIG. 3. TOMATO WORM.

long, slender tube, which serves for sucking up honey from the deep nectaries of flowers; the young of this moth is the great, disgusting, green "worm," or, more properly, caterpillar, which is furnished with a pair of strong, biting jaws. Thus we have an insect which, in one stage of its life, is a biting insect, and, in another stage, is a sucking insect.

This difference between the different stages of insect life tends to make the study of insects, as taken up by the economic entomologist, more difficult than at first sight it might appear to be. When we speak of biting insects, we must include in our minds not only those insects which, as adults, are biting, but we must have in mind, also, the young form of certain orders of insects which, as adults, are really sucking insects.

When we come to consider remedies, it is evident at once that remedies whose effectiveness consists in the fact that the foliage which is eaten by the insects is poisoned by being covered with a coating of some arsenical mixture cannot be used against sucking insects who get their food from the inside of the leaves. And it is evident that barriers around tree trunks, or around plats of ground, which might surely prevent the progress of the wingless caterpillars and worms, would not at all prevent the winged adult forms (the moths, etc.) of the insects — which adult forms lay the eggs from which the caterpillars are hatched — from getting into the tree tops, or into the plats of ground.

It is important to discover at what time in an insect's life remedies may be best applied; different remedies will be demanded by the different life-stages of the same insect. The life-stages of insects should be pretty fairly understood by anyone who hopes to carry on an intelligently-directed warfare with the insect pests of his farm or garden. First, there is the egg — deposited usually on the food-plant of the insect, so that the newly-hatched larvæ or caterpillars may run no risk of starving while hunting for their proper food. Often the insect may be veritably nipped in the bud, if we may become acquainted with its favorite place of oviposition, and destroy the eggs. Or, by protecting the plant, we may prevent the laying of eggs on it. (See recommendations for Spring Canker-worm.)

The second stage is, in insects which undergo a complete metamorphosis, the worm-like, caterpillar, grub or maggot stage, the young of various insects being thus variously termed. By entomologists this is called the larval stage, and the young, whether grub or maggot or caterpillar, is called the *larva*. This term will be used frequently in the succeeding pages, and its meaning should be remembered. In this stage most insect injury is done. The larvæ of moths and butterflies are the voracious caterpillars, as those of the Codlin Moth, the Tomato-worm, the Wheat-head Armyworm, the Garden Web-worm, the Fall Army-worm, the Spring Canker-worm, the Fall Web-worm, the Bag-worm, the Mapleworm, the Walnut-moth Worm, the Tussock-moth Worm, and the Clothes-moth Worm. The adult or moth forms of these insects are absolutely innoxious so far as devouring plant tissue goes, but from them come the eggs from which the ravaging larvæ issue.

The next stage is the pupal or chrysalid stage, in which the insect lies inactive within a hard protecting shell or case. This stage is passed either in the ground or in some place of shelter beneath stones, or boards, in crevices of bark, or even buried in seeds (as with the Pea- and Bean-weevils), or in the trunks of trees (as with the Apple-tree Borer). The changing from the larval stage to this quiescent or pupal stage is called *pupation*,

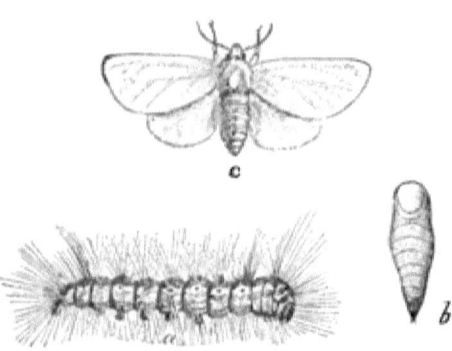

FIG. 4. FALL WEB-WORM MOTH, an insect which undergoes "complete metamorphosis;" *a*, larval form; *b*, pupal form; *c*, adult or moth form.

or, the larva is said to *pupate*. These terms are frequently used hereafter. During this stage the insect takes no food, but is undergoing within its protecting case the marvelous changes in bodily structure which result in the issuance of the beautiful white- and rose-tinted moth, with its four wings and delicate sucking tube, from a chrysalis which was formed by the pupation of the crawling, biting, sluggish, green Maple-worm.

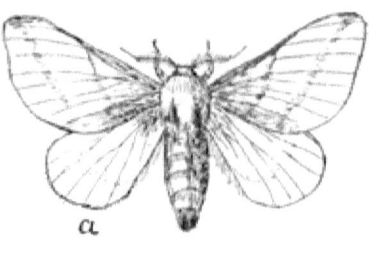

FIG. 5. MAPLE WORM; *a*, adult or moth; *b*, larva or "worm."

The fourth stage is that of the adult insect; the one real mission of which is the perpetuation of the species. As before said, no injury is done by the adult moths and butterflies, nor by the four-winged hymenopterous insects, (the Raspberry- and Rose-slug Saw-flies,) but many beetles are seriously injurious in the adult stage, as the Cucumber Beetle and others.

All insects, however, do not undergo such a complete metamorphosis, and four distinct stages cannot be made out in the lives of many. The grasshoppers, crickets, and cockroaches, and the sucking bugs, including the Chinch-bug and Squash-bug and the plant-lice, do not have a quiescent pupal stage. The young, when hatched from the egg, resemble the parent form, having the same

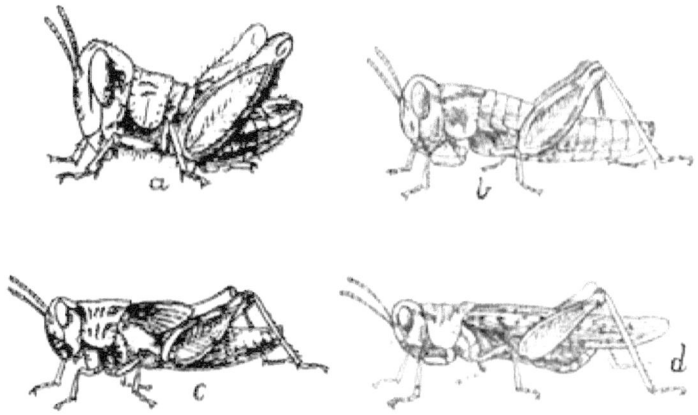

FIG. 6. ROCKY MOUNTAIN LOCUST, an insect which undergoes "incomplete metamorphosis;" *a, b, c,* young forms; *d,* adult.

kind of mouth-parts, but lacking wings. The wings soon begin to appear as small pads, which grow larger as the insect increases in size. The insect moults or casts its skin several times before reaching maturity, and at each moulting the wing-pads are seen to be considerably larger than before. The young of these insects sometimes differ in color from the adults, *e. g.,* young Chinch-bugs are red, the adults blackish. These insects are said to undergo an incomplete metamorphosis, the immature forms being active all the time, feeding all the time, and, what is important to us, injurious all the time. We are talking now, of course, of injurious species.

It is necessary, then, to know something of the structural characters and the life-history of each insect pest with which we wish to cope. Where and when are the eggs laid? What are the characters and habits of the young? What is the duration of the larval stage? Where and when does pupation take place? duration of pupal state? time of appearance and egg-laying of adults? in what life-stage does the insect hibernate? These and many other questions are to be answered before the economic entomologist can see his way to the most feasible method of fighting the insect pest under consideration.

In the succeeding pages the life-history and characters of each pest considered are briefly given. The *rationale* of the remedies proposed is thus made plain, and suggestions may come to some looking to the discovery of new remedies, or to the application of others not mentioned. The "Diagnoses" will serve to determine the specific pest which may be at work in the grain, vegetable or fruit attacked. I have included in the diagnoses the characteristics of the injury done, as well as the prominent characters of the insect pest in that life-stage in which the injury is done. The diagnoses may nearly serve as a sort of key for the determination of the 50 and more insect pests discussed. As to remedies, in order to save a tiresome repetition, and more especially to economize space, I have, in the following chapter, considered each of the more important insecticides in some detail, defining their character and giving approved methods of preparation and application. Under the head "Remedies" for each insect pest, the names of the suitable insecticides to be used are given, referring to the special chapter on remedies for the necessary information as to mode of use. The "Kansas Notes," finally, will be of interest to inquiring minds, and may be of some use to working entomologists.

REMEDIES.

Remedies for the ravages of injurious insects may be conveniently grouped under two heads: preventive remedies and active remedies. Among the preventive remedies are classed such measures as early seeding (see Wheat Midge) and late seeding (see Hessian Fly), the rotation of crops (see Corn-root Worm), protecting plants by screens (see Cucumber Beetle), mechanical barriers (see Spring Canker-worm), repellant washes (see Apple-tree Borer), and other means of preventing the laying of eggs on the food-plant or the accession of the living pests to the plant. The active remedies include those measures taken for the direct destruction of the pests, such as hand-picking (see Tomato-worm), trapping (see Squash-bug), crushing or burning (see Injurious Grasshoppers), or the use of insecticides.

The intelligent use of insecticidal substances by agriculturists and horticulturists is the means of a great annual saving. The most prominent apple-grower in Kansas, whose annual sales of fruit amount to nearly $50,000, attributes his remarkable success in fruit-growing largely to the liberal use of insecticides. His spraying operations are conducted on a scale commensurate with his extensive orchards, and his results attest the great value if not actual necessity of an intelligent warfare against insect pests carried on by the fruit-raiser.

The insecticides in present use may be considered under two heads: First, the internal poisons, taking effect by being eaten with the ordinary food of the insect; second, the external irritants, taking effect by closing the breathing pores (insects do not breathe through their mouths, but by means of small holes, a row of which is situated on each side of the body), or by extreme irritation of the body tissues.

The most important of the *internal poisons* are the arsenical poisons, Paris green and London purple.

PARIS GREEN, or arsenite of copper, containing 55 per cent. to 60 per cent. of insoluble arsenic, retailing at drug stores at about 23 cents a pound. For spraying (see directions and information as to machines, page 10), the Paris green should be mixed (it is insoluble, and only a mechanical mixture is obtained) with water, in the proportion of one pound to 150 to 200 gallons of water. The proportion, however, must vary with varying conditions of spraying. If the poison is applied too strong to the foliage of plants it is very destructive. The susceptibility to the influence of the poison varies in different plants. The foliage of peach trees is very easily injured, and the proportion of Paris green to water should not exceed one pound to 300 gallons. For apple, plum, and cherry, one pound to 200 gallons is safe, and yet effective in killing the insects. The corrosive power of the poisons may be much lessened if a quart of common flour for every 12 gallons of water is introduced into the mixture (Riley). In spraying the same trees several times during a season, the later applications should not be as strong as the earlier ones (Fletcher). In making the poisonous mixture, the Paris green should be mixed up with a small amount of water, as a paste, and the bulk of the water then added. The mixing must be effectively done; a thorough churning, by use of a force-pump, does it well; and during the spraying the mixture should be kept well stirred. The Paris green is rather heavy, and soon sinks to the bottom if left long undisturbed.

LONDON PURPLE, a by-product obtained in the manufacture of aniline dyes, containing a large percentage of arsenite of lime, and, in addition, some soluble arsenious acid. The total arsenic percentage is about the same as in Paris green. London purple is lighter and more finely divided than Paris green, and hence remains in suspension better in the water. The soluble arsenic, however, renders the danger of scorching the foliage more real; but the addition of lime will prevent almost all injury to foliage (Gillette). One pound of London purple to 200 gallons of water, with a pail or two of milk of lime, is recommended as the most approved formula (Smith). London purple costs less than Paris green, retailing at drug stores at about 15 cents a pound.

Either Paris green or London purple may be used dry. The poison should be mixed with 100 times its weight of perfectly dry land-plaster, air-slaked lime, flour, or sifted wood ashes, and dusted on the foliage (Fletcher).

The most important *external irritant* is a

KEROSENE EMULSION. Kerosene is a contact poison, possessing great penetrating powers. It has long been known, used pure, as a powerful insecticide, but its strength made it as dangerous to foliage as to the insects. Prepared as an emulsion, however, it is safe as regards foliage, and yet effective as an insect-killing substance. The emulsion should be prepared by the following formula:

Hard soap .... ½ pound.
Water .... 1 gallon.
Kerosene .... 2 gallons.

The soap should be dissolved in boiling hot water, and the suds poured, boiling hot, into the kerosene. The suds and kerosene should be thoroughly churned (preferably by means of a force-pump) until the emulsion is well made. It should appear as a rich, creamy mass. As it cools it thickens, jelly-like. When using, this stock emulsion should be diluted with from 9 to 12 times its measure of water. Thus, one gallon of stock emulsion will make 10 gallons of the emulsion ready to be sprayed. The emulsion is used against insects which cannot be killed by the use of arsenical poisons, such as plant-lice, scale insects, and various sucking bugs.

PYRETHRUM, a vegetable insect poison, acting by external contact. It is got by pulverizing the flowers of certain species of *Pyrethrum*. Its essential poisonous principle is a volatile oil, which escapes on the long standing of the powder. It is therefore absolutely necessary that fresh pyrethrum be obtained if any favorable results are to be expected. The reason for so many reported failures in using pyrethrum as an insecticide is undoubtedly found in the fact that stale powder was used. Persian Insect Powder, California Buhach, Dalmatian Insect Powder, are other names for pyrethrum. In inquiring at the druggist's, one should ask for fresh California Buhach, and for the best, and should insist on the freshness and the quality. While the powder is extremely active in its destructive effects on insects, it is practically harmless to human beings and household animals. The powder should be mixed with twice its bulk of rye flour, and kept in tight jars for two or three days, when the entire mass will be as effective as the pure powder (Smith). Common flour may be used, and the proportion vary from two to five times the bulk of the pyrethrum. It should be dusted over the insect-infested foliage when the pests are at work, so that it will come in contact with the bodies at once. It soon loses its power when exposed to the atmosphere. It can also be used mixed with water, one ounce to two or three gallons of water.

Pyrethrum is especially available for work in gardens, greenhouses, and hot-houses, and in the house. Many household pests, as flies, mosquitos, and wasps, may be quickly affected by throwing a small quantity of the powder into the air of a room by means of an insect gun or bellows, or by igniting a small quantity (a teaspoonful) and allowing it to smoulder (Fletcher). Pyrethrum retails at about 50 cents a pound.

WHITE HELLEBORE, a vegetable insecticide, being the finely-powdered roots of *Veratrum album*, of the lily family. Its effects and mode of use are similar to those of pyrethrum. It is especially commended as a remedy for the slugs of the various Saw-flies (see Raspberry- and Rose-slugs). It costs, at retail, about 75 cents a pound.

BI-SULPHIDE OF CARBON, a powerful, highly inflammable and poisonous insect-killing substance. It is very volatile, and its fumes are deadly to insect life. It is especially available for destroying insects attacking stored grain, where the fumes can be made to permeate the contents of a tight bin. In using it, extreme care should be taken that no burning substance, lighted lamp, lantern, etc., be brought near it while being used. It is a liquid, being put up in one-pound cans, which retail for about 25 cents each.

Tobacco, benzine, gasoline, carbolic acid, naphthaline, fish-oil soaps, lime, gas-tar, etc., are all insecticides of greater or less value, and available under various conditions. Wherever special remedies are recommended in this little manual, directions for their use will be found.

SPRAYING AND DUSTING.

The successful application of the Paris green and London purple mixtures and the kerosene emulsion on a large scale to fruit trees and small-fruit bushes and vegetables is a matter of much importance. Spraying outfits are of all grades of effectiveness and price. Anyone purposing to purchase a spraying outfit should write to various firms for their catalogues and lists, and decide for himself what outfit will best serve his purpose. The following firms manufacture outfits for spraying and dusting:

FIELD FORCE-PUMP COMPANY, Lockport, N. Y.
P. C. LEWIS, Catskill, N. Y.
M. J. CASWELL, Box 17, Sandusky, Ohio.
GOULDS MANUFACTURING COMPANY, Seneca Falls, N. Y.
NIXON NOZZLE AND MACHINE COMPANY, Dayton, Ohio.
THOS. WOODASON, 451 E. Cambria st., Philadelphia, Pa.
ALBINSON & TRUSHEIM, 2026 Fourteenth st., Washington, D. C.
ADAM WEABER, Vineland. N. J.
LEGGETT & BRO., 301 Pearl st., New York.

The essential points in a spraying outfit are a good force-pump and a good nozzle, which will project the liquid in a fine, evenly-divided spray. If little work is to be done, an ordinary force-pump with a piece of rubber hose and a spray nozzle will answer the purpose. If a considerable amount of spraying is to be done, specially adapted machinery should be used. Those pumps having the parts that come in contact with the liquid made of brass are the most durable, and although more expensive than those made of iron, the extra cost is a small item when the difference in durability is considered (Beckwith). For work in gardens or where low plants are to be sprayed, "knapsack sprayers," consisting of a thin copper tank holding from four to five gallons of the spraying mixture, with light force-pump attachment, are sufficient. For general orchard work, a machine mounted on wheels or arranged to be carried in a wagon is needed. The Riley or Cyclone and the Nixon are the best nozzles to use.

For applying dry insecticides, machines such as Leggett's Paris green gun or the Woodason bellows should be used. By means of a revolving fan blower or by other means, the powder is forced out in a perfect dust-cloud.

Home-made contrivances may be used to a limited extent; but they are likely to be not only ineffective, but, in the end, more costly than specially-prepared machines. Mr. James Fletcher, entomologist to the Canadian Department of Agriculture, says, on this point:

After considerable experience, I have come to the conclusion that it will repay anyone who has to apply insecticides to go to the expense of procuring a pair of proper bellows for dry mixtures, and a force-pump for liquid applications. Such make-shift contrivances as ordinary watering cans, whisks, wisps of hay, or bunches of leaves, which are frequently used, actually cost far more in wasted time and materials than would pay for the best special instruments; added to which, when the work is done, it is neither satisfactory nor effective.

Some objection has been made to the use of arsenical poisons on fruit-trees, but repeated experiments by careful men have conclusively proved the absence of sound basis for this objection. Arsenic is not absorbed by fruits or plants, and as the applications are made while the fruit is very small, giving opportunity for the minute quantity of poison to be washed off by rains and blown off by winds, no danger is incurred.

PREVENTION.

As elsewhere, an "ounce of prevention is worth a pound of cure" in fighting insects. Preventive remedies are the surest, cheapest, and, at present, least used of all remedial measures. It seems wasteful to fight bugs when there are apparently no bugs to fight. High cultivation is the most general preventive remedy. A weak plant inevitably succumbs to the attacks of insects sooner than a strong plant. The many natural enemies of the various insect pests will often prove effective in saving the crop, if the crop can maintain itself against the invaders long enough for the massing of these enemies against the destructive insect species. The time that a crop can maintain itself in the face of insect attack certainly varies with the condition of the crop at the time of the attack. A well-fed, healthy crop will stand more than a starved one.

Cleanliness of the farm, garden or orchard is an important preventive remedy. Many noxious insects hibernate, as adults, in brush heaps and rubbish of various kinds. This is especially true of the Hemiptera, the sucking bugs. Early or late seeding and crop rotation are evidently preventive remedies, and, where applicable, usually the most effective of any remedies available.

Covering the trunks of fruit trees with an alkaline or poisonous wash, to prevent the attacks of borers; coating young apples with arsenic, to prevent the young Codlin Moth larvæ from getting into the fruit; mechanical contrivances to prevent the laying of eggs on the food-plant, or the access of the insect in its destructive stage, such as covering plants with screens and encircling tree trunks with barriers, to prevent the ascent of foliage-eaters, are preventive remedies of a "deterrent" (Fletcher) nature.

INSECTS ATTACKING CEREAL CROPS.

CORN INSECTS.

CHINCH-BUG.
(*Blissus leucopterus* Say; Order, Hemiptera.)

Diagnosis.—A small dark-colored bug with white wings, a dark triangular spot on each, in great numbers on the corn stalks and growing leaves, sucking the juices from the plant; the corn turns yellow and withers. The bugs are often in such numbers as to blacken considerable spaces on the corn plants.

Attacking also wheat, millet, and other cereals, and grasses.

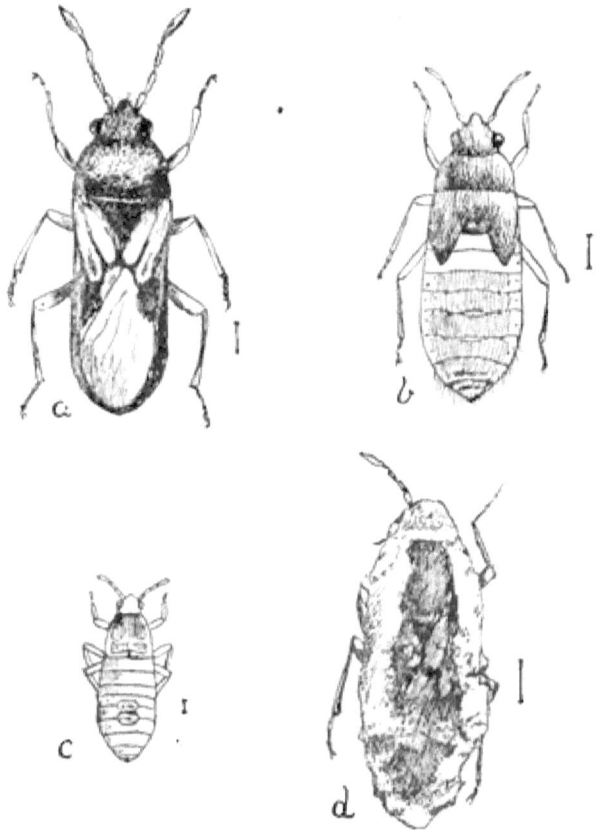

FIG. 7. CHINCH-BUG; *a*, adult; *b*, young with prominent wing-pads; *c*, very young or "red bug;" *d*, adult killed by the *Sporotrichum* fungus and covered by it.

Description and Life-history.—The Chinch-bug is unfortunately a familiar object to Kansas farmers. It is when adult about one-sixth of an inch in length, four-winged, the two front wings white, with a small triangular black dot about the middle of the outer margin. The young resemble the adult in general shape, but lack wings, or have merely short wing-pads. When very young the bugs are bright red. The bug is injurious in all stages, young, half-grown, and adult.

The eggs are laid in the spring (from middle of March to middle of May) by bugs which have hibernated in the adult stage. The eggs are laid a few at a time, perhaps 500 being laid by each female. The young "red bugs" begin work in the wheat fields, and usually remain in the wheat until harvest (last of June to middle of July), when the destructive host moves into the fields of young and growing corn. It requires about six weeks for the maturing of the bugs. The adults now pair and the cycle of a new generation begins. The perfect insects of this generation are those which pass through the winter and lay the eggs the following spring for the next year's first brood. It is highly probable if not certain that a third brood often appears in Kansas.

The Chinch-bug, though winged, uses its powers of flight but little, and its migrations from wheat to corn fields in July are usually on foot. The wings are used to some degree at pairing time.

Remedies.—The gathering together of all rubbish, old corn stalks, dead leaves, etc., in which old bugs pass the winter, and burning it, will destroy many parent bugs, thereby largely lessening the spring brood.

High cultivation, to enable the plants to withstand the attacks of the pests.

Disputing the entrance of the bugs into the field, when migrating on foot, by plowing furrows around the field and pouring coal-tar into the ditches.

There are several natural remedies, namely, the attacks of predaceous insects, as aphis-lions, lady-birds, and others, and the attacks of some birds, as the common quail.

Most effective of all, however, has proved the artificial dissemination of contagious diseases among the bugs. The practical application of this method, which has been attended with marked and gratifying success, is to be credited to Prof. F. H. Snow, of this Department. His experiments have been carried on for three years, and the arrangements for spreading the diseases over the State, whenever the Chinch-bugs appear, are very complete.

The diseases are caused by the parasitic growth on or in the bugs of at least two different fungi (*Sporotrichum globuliferum* Spegazinni) and *Empusa aphidis* Hoffman) and one bacterial form (*Micrococcus insectorum* Burrill). The remedy is effective for the same reason that if, in time of war, enemies were to send into a large city, as New York, men sick with the small-pox or Asiatic cholera, the infection would rapidly spread among the massed people of the city and wholesale destruction of life would result. So with the Chinch-bugs massed in the Kansas corn fields, when dying and dead bugs bearing with them the germs and spores of contagious diseases are introduced. For a full and exhaustive account of the experiments in this line, under Professor Snow's direction, reference should be made to the "First Annual Report of the Director of the Experimental Station of the University of Kansas, April, 1892," 230 pp., four plates, which will be sent on application, accompanied by 7 cents for postage, to this Department. Infected bugs will be sent to any farmer in the State applying for them. The following directions for obtaining and using the infected bugs are quoted from Professor Snow's report:

In order to keep up our supply of infected bugs, we must require that each person sending for infection send us live bugs from the field. These should be put into a tin box (a baking-powder box is excellent for this purpose), *without soil*, and with a supply of green wheat or corn. The box should have a tight-fitting cover, and no holes need to be made. We have found that the bugs reach us in the best condition when sent us in this way.

Upon receipt of infected bugs from the station, a shallow box about 24x36x6 inches, with tight joints, should be provided. Sprinkle the whole inside of the box with water and put in enough green wheat or corn to cover the bottom. Scatter the infected bugs over the bottom and put in a large quantity of live bugs from the field; a quart would not be too many for a box of the size above suggested. A smaller box may be used for a smaller quantity of bugs. After the bugs have remained in the box two days, remove half of them, alive and dead, and scatter them over that part of the field where the bugs are thickest; at the same time replenish the infection box with more bugs from the field. Continue to scatter bugs from the infection box over the field at intervals of two days, until it is seen that the bugs are dying rapidly all over the field. Keep the box moist by repeated sprinkling and change the green food as often as it loses its freshness.

Careful attention to these directions will often insure success where careless use of the infection would fail. Make daily notes on the appearance of the bugs in the infection box and in the field, and of the weather while the field infection is in progress. Note carefully the Chinch-bug conditions in neighboring fields. Keep a list of farmers who get infected bugs from your field.

Save a quantity of fungus covered and non-fungus-covered dead bugs in a tin box for use the following year. Put the infection box away for future use.

Should the first lot of infected bugs from the station seem to fail in their purpose, send without delay for a new supply.

Do not fail to send a full report of the experiment to the director of the station.

Kansas Notes.—The Chinch-bug was first known in the Mississippi valley in 1823. (See S. A. Forbes, in Insect Life, Vol. I, No. 8, p. 249.)

I am unable to find matter showing the time of the first recognition of the Chinch-bug as a pest in Kansas. In 1871 Wm. Le Baron, State Entomologist, of Illinois, writing to the *Prairie Farmer* (August 5), says that hosts of Chinch-bugs "have devastated the fields of spring wheat and barley all through the central counties of Illinois, and also in parts of Iowa, Missouri, Kansas, and the southern border of Nebraska."

Townend Glover, U. S. Entomologist, in the report of the U. S. Commissioner of Agriculture for 1871, states that the Chinch-bug has been very destructive in Iowa, Kansas, and the Northwestern States.

Beginning with 1873, the *Prairie Farmer* continuously refers, by means of letters from correspondents, to the presence of the Chinch-bug in greater or less numbers in Kansas.

In the report of the U. S. Commissioner of Agriculture for 1874, Mr. Glover reports that 27 Kansas counties sustained losses from Chinch-bugs.

I have been able to find enough data on Chinch-bug occurrence since 1883 to say that the Chinch-bugs did not occur in alarming numbers in 1884 and 1885; that they were present in force in 1886, 1887, and 1888; not present in 1889 and 1890, and were present in 1891 and 1892.

WESTERN CORN-ROOT WORM.

(*Diabrotica longicornis* Say; Order, Coleoptera.)

Diagnosis.—Stalks of corn wilt; fall over easily, a strong wind blowing down many. In the roots and in the soil about the roots are to be found small (¼ to ½ inch long) white six-legged grubs.

Description and Life-history.—The adult is a small beetle about one-fourth inch long, plain greenish-brown to grass green, without spots or stripes, belonging to the leaf-eating family Chrysomelidæ. The eggs are laid in the ground in the fall near the

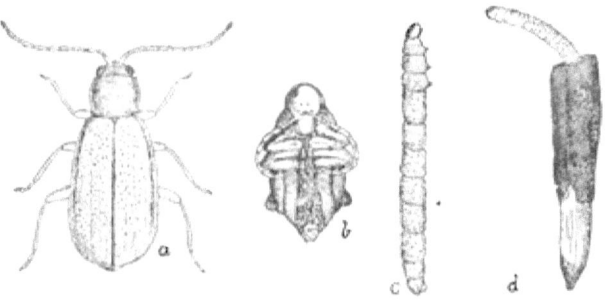

FIG. 5. WESTERN CORN-ROOT WORM. *a*, adult; *b*, pupa; *c*, larva; *d*, larva in corn root.

roots of corn. The larvæ or "worms" are hatched in May and June, after the ground has been plowed and planted to corn. It is in this worm stage that the injury is done. The worm is from one-fourth to one-half inch long, six-legged, soft, and white, with a small brown head. The worms burrow into the roots of corn, eating their way upward. As many as 15 or 20 may attack a single hill. The corn is stunted in growth, and because of the loss of its roots topples over easily. Many stalks will not be two feet high; others of the usual height will form no ears; and some will hardly tassel.

Remedies.—So far as at present known, the insect has no other food-plant than corn, and this suggests at once an effective remedy, namely, the rotation of crops and consequent starving of the insect. The eggs being laid in the fall in the corn field, it is evident that, if some other crop than corn be planted on the ground the next spring, the larvæ hatching in May and June will be starved to death.

High cultivation is, of course, beneficial in strengthening attacked corn, which may be able to send out new roots to replace those destroyed by the insect. In moist, rich ground the corn will probably successfully resist ordinary attacks of the worm. From their subterranean situation, the larvæ cannot be got at by birds.

Kansas Notes.—This corn pest has been known in Kansas for 10 years or more. Prof. E. A. Popenoe called attention to it in 1883 (Third Biennial Report Kansas State Board of Agriculture, 1881-'82, p. 616), as at work "in the corn lands along the Kaw valley." Professor Snow reported its presence in 1885 (Report of Kansas State Board of Agriculture for quarter ending December 31, 1885). A correspondent from Johnson county, quoted by Professor Snow, declares that a 20-acre field of corn will not make 15 bushels per acre because of the ravages of the pest.

In 1891 several specimens of the insect and reports of its ravages were received by this Department. A correspondent in Coffey county wrote: "They have been in our field for several years. . . . This year they have spread so rapidly that it is alarming."

Mr. S. J. Hunter, a student of this Department, reports the presence of the pest in damaging numbers this year in the vicinity of Greeley, Anderson county. One-third of a field of 30 acres is damaged to the extent of one-half the crop. The piece has been in corn for six consecutive years. An adjoining field of 14 acres will yield but one-third of a crop because of the ravages of the pest. On Mr. Hunter's own field of 35 acres, fully 5 per cent. of the corn plants are infested. Several other fields in the vicinity have been seriously damaged. The loss in this neighborhood, this year, will amount to several hundred dollars. All of the attacked fields have been planted to corn for several consecutive years.

SOUTHERN CORN-ROOT WORM.

(*Diabrotica 12-punctata* Oliv.; Order, Coleoptera.)

Diagnosis.—Same as for Western Corn-root Worm.

Description and Life-history.—The larva, or "worm," cannot easily, if at all, be distinguished from the Western Corn-root Worm. The adult is a small, yellow beetle, with 12 black spots on its back (wing covers), and with a black head. This insect is closely allied to the Western Corn-root Worm, but differs from it in feeding upon a great variety of vegetation, garden crops as well as corn being attacked. It has a more southern habitat than the western form. It is also two-brooded, "eggs for the first brood being deposited in spring, about the roots of young corn; the second brood usually developing upon the roots of certain wild plants, especially those of the Compositæ family."

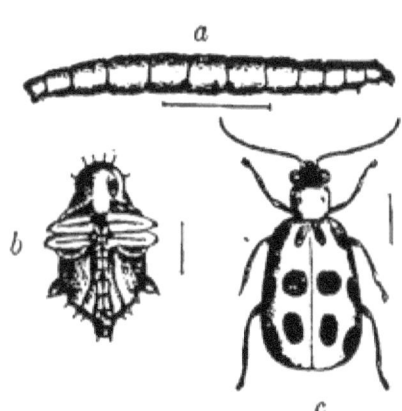

FIG. 9. SOUTHERN CORN-ROOT WORM; *a*, larva; *b*, pupa; *c*, adult.

Remedies.—As this insect is not restricted to one food-plant, it cannot be starved out. So far, no practicable remedy has been found for this pest in its corn-infesting stage. As recommended for the Western Corn-root Worm, high cultivation will aid the corn in resisting the attacks of the pest.

Kansas Notes.—In 1891 a correspondent in Bourbon county sent in specimens of the adult beetle. The correspondent believed that his corn was being injured by this pest. Mr. S. J. Hunter found a few specimens of *12-punctata* in Anderson county fields infested with *longicornis*. (See Western Corn-root Worm.)

I have this year seen many specimens in a Lyon county cornfield.

CORN-ROOT LOUSE.

(*Aphis maidi-radicis* Forbes; Order, Hemiptera.)

Diagnosis. — Corn plants grow slowly, or not at all; appear yellow and sickly. Examination of the roots reveals small bluish-green particles, masses of lice.

Description and Life-history. — This minute insect, one of the plant-lice, has until lately been believed to be a root form of the Corn-louse which lives above ground on the leaves and stalks.

FIG. 10. CORN-ROOT LOUSE: *a*, winged female; *b*, wingless female (stem-mother); *c*, wingless, egg-laying female; *d*, pupa.

Professor Forbes, of Illinois, has clearly shown the distinctiveness of the two forms. With proper magnification by a microscope, the Corn-root Louse appears as a wingless, soft-bodied, bluish-green, sub-ovoid insect; or it may have four transparent membranous wings.

The louse passes the winter in the egg state in the nests of certain small, brown ants (*Lasius brunneus* var. *alienus*), which ants are always found associated with the lice. The young lice hatch in April, and begin to feed upon the roots of young smart-weed plants (*Polygonum*); and later upon the common crab-grass (*Setaria*). As soon, however, as the corn is planted and begins growing, the lice go to the corn roots, and there live. In October the eggs for next year's generation are laid.

Remedies. — As the young lice are usually hatched before the corn is planted, and have to live on other plant roots, as smart-weed and crab-grass, any means for keeping down the sprouting herbage in the fields in early spring will tend to starve the young lice. It has been found that the young lice cannot live more than five days without food. "Any treatment of the field the preceding summer or fall which should diminish the number of seeds of pigeon grass or smart-weed maturing in the corn would diminish likewise the chances of survival of young root-lice the following year."

Kansas Notes.—This insect has not been very generally observed in the State, but it is undoubtedly more common than indicated by the lack of observations.

CORN-LOUSE.

(*Aphis maidis* Fitch; Order, Hemiptera.)

Diagnosis.—Many minute soft, green insects on the stalks, leaves, or tassels; small brown ants running up and down the stalks; wilting of the corn leaves.

Description and Life-history.—Very small, soft-bodied, apple-green insects; body elliptical or slightly ovate in outline. The

FIG. 11. CORN-LOUSE; *a*, winged female; *b*, pupa; *c*, wingless female.

insects are mostly wingless, though in the late fall winged specimens may be found. The eggs are laid in the fall and hatch the following spring.

Remedies.—There are so many natural enemies of the plant-lice that they are rarely permitted to do serious damage, despite their extraordinary prolificness. Several species of lady-beetles feed on the Corn-louse. The lice could be easily destroyed by the use of kerosene emulsion (see p. 9), but this would be impracticable as a general remedy in fields.

Kansas Notes.—Prof. E. A. Popenoe found this insect attacking cane in southern Kansas in 1882.

A correspondent in Brown county wrote this Department under date of June 2, 1891, sending specimens of the louse and reporting its attacks on sprouting corn. The correspondent said: "When the corn is almost through the ground, the lice collect on the sprout as thick as they can possibly hang, when in a day or two the sprout withers and dies." Specimens were taken in a corn field in Riley county, August 1, this year (1892).

ROCKY MOUNTAIN LOCUST.
(*Melanoplus spretus* Thomas; Order, Orthoptera.)

Diagnosis.—A locust or grasshopper, measuring from head to tip of front wings (folded) about $1\frac{1}{4}$ inches, never reaching $1\frac{1}{2}$ inches. Appears in great numbers and attacks all vegetation, preferably cereals and vegetables.

Attacking also almost all farm and garden produce, shade-trees, shrubs, flowers, and grasses.

Description and Life-history.—The adult is dirty olive and brown; front wings with a rather faint row of dirty brown spots extending along the middle from base to tip. Hind wings transparent, uncolored; tibiæ of hind legs red. The young resemble the adult, except in the matter of wings; the very young have no wings; older ones have short, pad-like wings, incapable of flight. The adult locusts appear in the summer or fall, coming from the northwest in great swarms; the young appear, if at all, in the spring following fall invasion. The natural home of this pest is on the high plains of northwest United States, but its migratory habits bring it to Kansas. Since 1876, however, it has not appeared in serious numbers. It is a matter of importance to distinguish between this migratory and alien form and the Reg-legged Locust (*Melanoplus femur-rubrum*), which is native to the State and does no appreciable harm to cereals. The two species closely resemble each other in appearance, but the Rocky Mountain form has the front wings when folded projecting at least one-third of their length beyond the tip of the abdomen, while in the Red-legged Locust the front wings just reach the tip of the abdomen, or project very slightly. The last joint of the abdomen of the males in the Rocky Mountain species is turned up like the prow of a canoe and is notched so that two small tubercles appear; in the Red-legged Locust the last joint of the male abdomen is broader and not narrowed and not notched, appearing, as Dr. Riley has said, more like the stern of a barge. The males of either species may be distinguished from

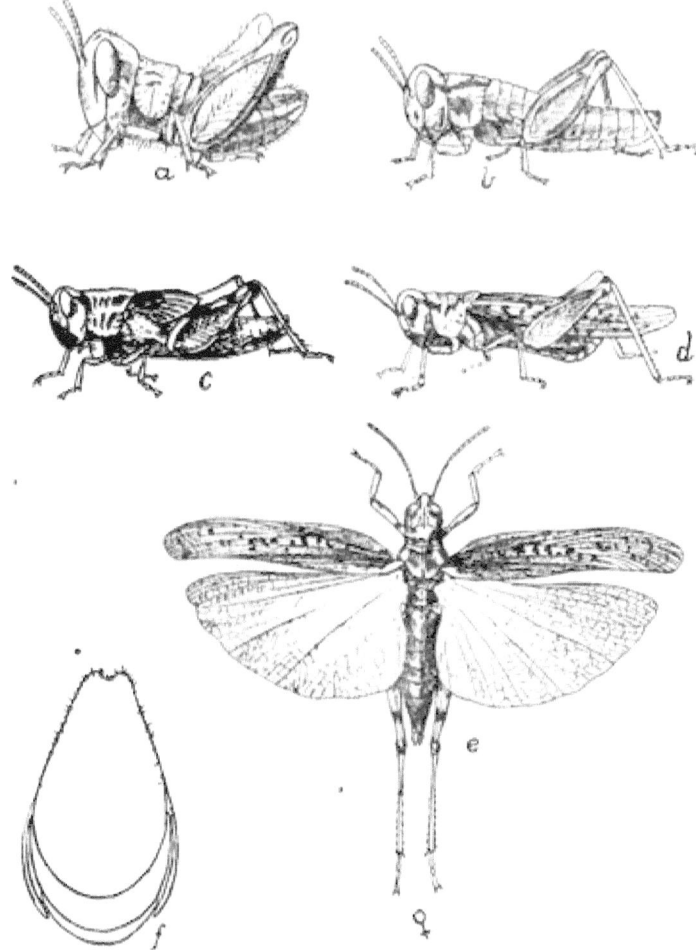

FIG. 12. ROCKY MOUNTAIN LOCUST: *a*, very young; *b*, young; *c*, young with wing-pads; *d*, adult; *e*, adult female; *f*, terminal view of last abdominal segment of male.

the females by the lack of an ovipositor or egg-laying apparatus; this ovipositor appearing as four small, pointed, backward-projecting pieces, which may be spread apart or closely pressed together.

The eggs of locusts or grasshoppers are laid in the ground in masses of from 50 to 100, and the young when first hatched are, as previously stated, without wings.

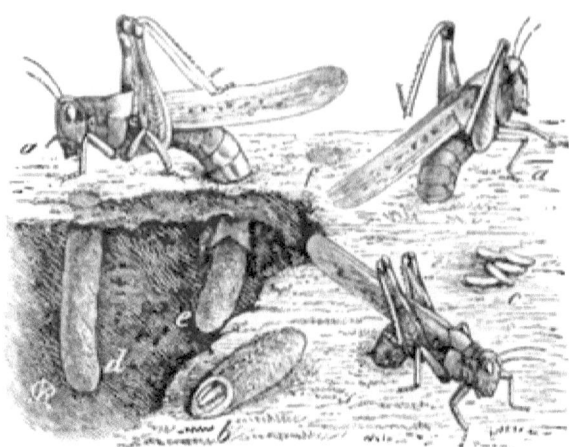

FIG. 13. ROCKY MOUNTAIN LOCUST; *a, a, a*, females laying eggs; *b*, egg-pod with broken end, taken from ground; *c*, eggs taken from pod; *d, e*, egg-pods in place below surface of ground; *f*, place where an egg-pod is buried.

Remedies.—There are several natural enemies of the Rocky Mountain Locust which do good work in keeping the pest down. A minute, red mite fastens itself on the body near the base of the wings and sucks its blood; several flies are parasitic upon it, and birds eat the locusts with relish. The artificial remedies are most effective when applied to the young or unfledged (wingless) locusts, and will be discussed under the head of "Injurious Grasshoppers."

Kansas Notes.—The State was invaded by the Rocky Mountain Locust in 1866. In 1868 a few (comparatively) locusts descended in Riley county. In 1874 another great invasion occurred, and the next spring much harm was done by young hatching from eggs deposited the previous fall by the invaders. As soon as these young acquired wings, however, about June 1, they flew away to the northwest, attempting to return to their native habitat. In 1876 fresh swarms appeared from the northwest, and great injury was done.

We have now gone so long without hearing from our voracious friends of the northwest, that it is probable that changed conditions, such as the increase of the food-supply in their breeding region, etc., render unnecessary any further straying from home in search of Kansas corn. It is certainly most devoutly to be hoped that such is the case.

An occasional "grasshopper scare" in western Kansas keeps alive the remembrance of the early troubles, but these "scares" are always found to be caused by the unusual prevalence of some local species, and not due to the presence of the true Rocky Mountain Locust. Concerning these other locust species, which occasionally do more or less harm, see chapter on "Injurious Grasshoppers."

GARDEN WEB-WORM.

(*Eurycreon rantalis* Guenée; Order, Lepidoptera.)

Diagnosis.—White webs enveloping the young corn or the bases of the older corn stalks. Within the webs numbers of slender, light-green, black-dotted caterpillars eating the leaves.

Attacking, also, many garden vegetables and wild plants.

Description and Life-history.—The insect in the state in which it commits its depredations is a caterpillar or lepidopterous larva, about seven-eighths of an inch long when full grown. It is light

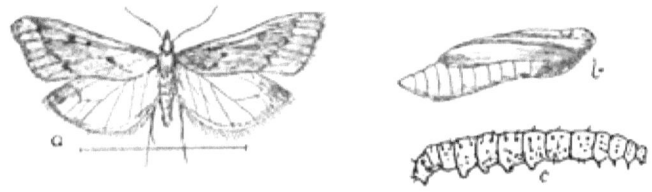

FIG. 14. GARDEN WEB-WORM; *a*, adult; *b*, pupa; *c*, larva.

green, with a narrow, yellowish-white stripe on each side of the median dorsal line except on the first segment behind the head. Head pale yellowish-red. There are eight pairs of legs, the last pair being on the last segment of the caterpillar.

As an adult, the insect is a small, grayish, night-flying moth, its wings expanding about three-fourths to one inch. The eggs are deposited on the lower leaves and stems of various plants. The larvæ become full grown in about two weeks after hatching, and transform into pupæ within a small, silken cocoon concealed under dead leaves or in any debris.

The larva feeds naturally on certain wild plants and weeds, especially the different species of pig-weeds, lambs-quarter, and purslane. When the larvæ are very abundant, however, they overflow into fields and gardens. Many garden vegetables suffer equally with corn. Tomatoes, potatoes, cucumbers, lettuce, radishes, peas and turnips are attacked.

Remedies.—Corn planted early gets a start which enables it to resist the attacks of the caterpillar. Early planting may be said to be the surest safeguard. In infested gardens, fowls may be allowed to run. Spraying with some arsenical, as Paris green, or London purple (see p. 7.), where the poison can be used without endangering life, is effective. (For spraying directions, see page 10.)

Kansas Notes.—In the Second Biennial Report Kansas Board of Agriculture, 1879-'80, p. 493, Prof. E. A. Popenoe presented interesting notes on the occurrence of the Web-worm. In June of 1880 "fields and gardens in the central portion of the State suffered severely from the ravages" of this pest. Professor Popenoe bred a Tachinid fly from the caterpillar, and believed that this parasite was ordinarily present in sufficient force to be a considerable check upon the increase of the caterpillars.

In the report of the Kansas Board of Agriculture for the month ending June 30, 1885, Prof. F. H. Snow reports the presence of this insect in considerable numbers in 35 counties of the State, the counties most infested being confined to the southeastern quarter of the State. The chief injuries in 1880 were inflicted upon corn and potatoes. A complete list of the plants destroyed includes sweet-corn, field corn, Irish potatoes, sweet-potatoes, millet, flax, cotton, castor beans, clover, timothy, cabbage, peas, beets, lettuce, melons, cucumbers, onions, and other garden-stuff. The extent of the damage reached about 10 per cent. of the entire crop in the counties most seriously attacked.

In 1891 the Department received reports of the presence of the worm in Kiowa, Clark and Cowley counties. A correspondent in Kiowa county wrote as follows:

They form a web around our garden vegetables of almost every kind except potatoes, and completely destroy them. They are reported to-day [June 24] in field corn to considerable extent, destroying it in some places entirely.

Another correspondent, sending specimens June 26, writes:

Chrysanthemums, carnations, asters, pinks and geraniums are going; also a field of young corn.

CORN WORM.

(*Heliothis armigera* Hübner; Order, Lepidoptera.)

Diagnosis.—Greenish-brown, dark-striped caterpillar, an inch to an inch and a half long, feeding on the kernels of ripening sweet or field corn. Unsightly irregular channels are gnawed along the cob.

Attacking, also, the tomato.

Description and Life-history.—The adult is greenish-yellow, (front wings pale clay yellow, with a greenish tint, hind wings paler,) the forewings bearing each a conspicuous dark spot near

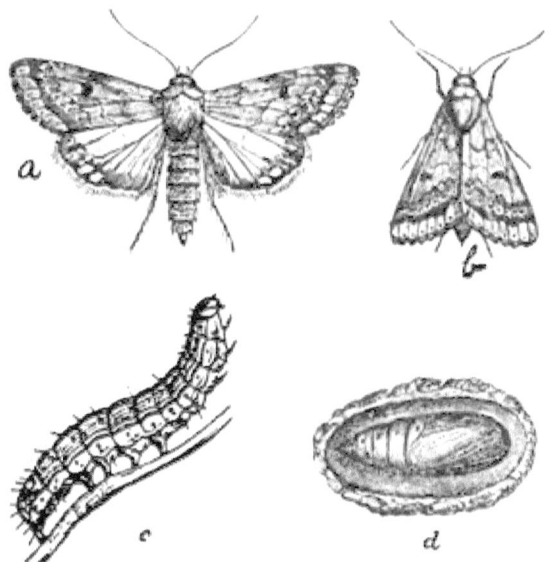

FIG. 15. CORN WORM: *a*, *b*, adult; *c*, larva; *d*, pupa, in cocoon.

the middle. The eggs are laid upon the silk of the young ears. "The larvæ soon hatch, and eat through the husk to the succulent kernels beneath, which they devour greedily for several weeks." The full-grown caterpillar is about 1½ inches long, and varies in color from pale green to dark brown, with darker longitudinal stripes. On each segment of the body there are eight circular, shining, black spots, from which arise short, brown hairs. The full-grown larvæ descend to the ground, burrow a few inches into the soil, and there form loose, oval cocoons of silk and dirt, within which they pupate. The adult moths issue in from two to four weeks. There are probably two broods in Kansas, the larvæ of the first paying special attention to early sweet-corn.

Remedies.—It is the very early (first brood) and very late (second brood) corn that suffers most, so that intermediately-ripening corn is apt to be comparatively free from attack. Hand-picking is the most available and effective remedy so far devised. "The silk of infested ears shows the presence of the larvæ by being prematurely dry or partially eaten, and the larvæ may be readily found and crushed. In garden patches of sweet-corn, at least, this method is worth using." Fall plowing of infested fields will break up and expose many pupæ.

Kansas Notes.—Dr. Riley, in his third annual report as State Entomologist of Missouri, says:

In 1860, the year of the great drouth in Kansas, the corn crop in that State was almost entirely ruined by the Corn-worm. According to the *Prairie Farmer* of January 31, 1861, one county there, which raised 436,000 bushels of corn in 1859, only produced 5,000 bushels of poor, wormy stuff in 1860; and this, we are told, was a fair sample of most of the counties in Kansas. . . . It appears, also, that many horses in Kansas subsequently died from disease, occasioned by having this half-eaten, wormy corn fed out to them.

OTHER INSECTS ATTACKING CORN.

Fall Army-worm.

Injurious Grasshoppers.

INSECTS ATTACKING CEREAL CROPS —Cont.

WHEAT INSECTS.

HESSIAN FLY.

(*Cecidomyia destructor* Say; Order, Diptera.)

Diagnosis.—The wheat plants turn yellow and die. In April and May very small, white grubs may be found in the sheathing-bases close to the ground; in the winter small, brown, oval, flax-seed-like bodies may be found in the plant near the roots.

Description and Life-history.—The adult insect is a small, blackish, two-winged fly with rather long, slender legs and beautiful, feathered antennæ. The adult, however, is rarely seen. The flies of each generation go through four distinct life-stages: (1) The egg, (2) the larva or grub, (3) the pupa or "flax-seed," (4) the adult or winged insect. In no other stage than the larval is any injury done to the wheat. Professor Forbes, of Illinois, has carefully studied the life-history of this pest, and the following summary account of the life-history of the insect is quoted from a bulletin issued by him in 1890:

There are always two destructive generations in a single year, and under some circumstances at least three. In fact, I have obtained evidence that there may be even four generations which attack the wheat with destructive effect, two in spring and two in autumn. The principal injuries, however, are done by the last autumnal and the first spring generations.

The eggs are a slender oval, about a fiftieth of an inch in length, and small enough to lie lengthwise in the grooves upon the upper surface of the leaf of the wheat. Those for the principal autumn brood of the maggots are laid most commonly on the leaf of the young wheat. The maggot hatching from these makes its way down the leaf to the base of its sheath, near the root, and here this milk-white, oval, smooth larva remains motionless until it gets its growth (commonly in November), after which it forms a tough, smooth, dark-brown case, within which it spends the winter, still in the same position. From this case (the "flax-seed" above mentioned) the winged insect bursts forth about the 1st of the following April, in the form of a delicate, nearly black, two-winged fly or gnat, which has a very close general resemblance to a small mos-

FIG. 16. HESSIAN FLY; a healthy stalk of wheat on the left, the one on the right dwarfed and the lower leaves beginning to wither and turn yellow; the stem swollen at three places near the ground, where the "flax-seeds" (h) are situated, between the stem and sheathing base of the leaf; a, egg greatly enlarged; b, larva enlarged; c, "flax-seed" or puparium case; d, pupa; e, adult, natural size, laying its eggs on the leaf; f, adult, female, enlarged; g, adult, male, enlarged; h, "flax-seed" between the leaves and stalk; i, Ichneumon parasite of the Hessian Fly, male, enlarged.

quito. The sexes pair at once, and the eggs for another generation are laid almost immediately in the field, the adults perishing soon thereafter.

The maggots hatching from these spring eggs go through the same course of development, at the base of the stalk, behind the sheath of the leaf, and do the principal part of the damage noticed in the spring, causing the well-known "crinkling" or falling down of the straw as the wheat heads out. Many of the winged flies of this brood hatch sometime before harvest, beginning to appear, in fact, by the end of May, and these lay eggs at once and give rise to a second spring brood—a fact clearly established this season by breeding experiments at Champaign. By harvest practically all are in the so-called "flax-seed" state, and the greater part of them remain behind in this condition in the stubble after the grain is cut. A few, however, are carried away with the straw. From these harvest-time "flax-seeds" the fall generations descend, the first of them appearing either in the volunteer grain or in early-sown wheat, and the second—the hibernating generation already referred to—in wheat of the regular crop. The laying of the eggs for the first of these generations certainly begins by September 1, and apparently somewhat earlier. The average length of life of one generation or brood (except the hibernating one), from any stage around to the same stage again, is about six weeks.

It is, however, a fact of considerable economic interest that this division into generations is not anywhere complete, but that "flax-seeds" of any generation may lie dormant during the whole life of a generation following, finally hatching with the descendants of their original contemporaries. Thus, of those "flax-seeds" which form in May and June, some may give the winged fly in June and July, and others not until September; and some of those which form in volunteer wheat in September may hibernate and emerge the following spring.

Remedies.—The United States Entomological Commission, in its third report (1883) suggests the following remedies:

1. There are several destructive Ichneumon parasites of the Hessian Fly, whose combined attacks are supposed at times to destroy about nine-tenths of all the flies hatched. Of these the most important is the Chalcid four-winged fly, *Semiotellus destructor*, which infests the "flaxseed," and a small parasite of the genus *Platygaster*.

2. By sowing a part of the wheat early, and, if affected by the fly, plowing this in and sowing the rest after September 20, the wheat crop may in most cases be saved. It should be remembered that the first brood should be circumvented, or destroyed, in order that a second or spring brood may not appear.

3. If the wheat be only partially affected, it may be saved by fertilizers and careful cultivation; or a badly damaged field of winter wheat may thus be recuperated in the spring.

4. Pasturing with sheep, and consequent close cropping of the wheat in November and early December, may cause many of the eggs, larvæ and flax-seeds to be destroyed; also, rolling the ground may have nearly the same effect.

5. Sowing hardy varieties. The Underhill Mediterranean wheat, and especially the Lancaster variety, which tillers vigorously, should be sown in preference to the slighter, less vigorous kinds, in a region much infested by the fly. The early- (August) sown wheat (to be plowed under afterward), might be Diehl; the later sown, Lancaster, Clawson, or Fultz.

6. Of special remedies, the use of lime, soot or salt may be recommended; also, raking off the stubble; but too close cutting of the wheat and burning the stubble are of doubtful use, as this destroys the useful parasites as well as the flies.

Professor Forbes, in the bulletin above referred to, offers the following as the most important general preventive and remedial measures:

1. As a large percentage of these insects remain in the stubble at harvest, in the "flax-seed state," and as the flies which hatch from them later are weak and delicate, the ground may well be plowed, as soon after harvest as practicable, and rolled to close the cracks through which the winged insects might escape. If the stubble can be made to burn, this will, of course, destroy the "flax-seeds" even more effectually.

2. The volunteer grain springing up in the fields must be closely watched, and measures taken to destroy it about four weeks after its appearance, as it will otherwise assist to carry the insect through the summer in undiminished or perhaps larger numbers. The most convenient method of doing this will depend so much upon the season and the cropping planned, that each must select his method for himself.

3. Such of the "flax-seeds" as are carried away in the grain may be destroyed by heating or burning the screenings from the thresher, if the wheat is threshed at once.

4. To prevent the wheat from becoming infested in fall by the first autumnal brood, and to escape as much as possible of the second, the sowing of the wheat may, with advantage, be postponed as late as is consistent with its reasonable safety from winter-killing — to the last of September or the first of October, according to the common practice in the southern half of Illinois.

5. The damage done by any but the severest kind of an attack will depend, other things being equal, on the fertility of the soil and the strength of the plant. If the latter be strong enough to send out from the root new and vigorous stalks to replace those killed by the maggots of the fly, a considerable amount of fly attack may be scarcely noticeable at harvest time. From this it follows that the maintenance of the fertility of the soil is often a measurable safeguard against loss. I have

no doubt that the soluble commercial fertilizers, applied in spring to infested fields, would have a happy effect, whether with profit or not can only be tested by experiment.

6. Finally, other things being equal, those varieties of wheat with a stiff and flinty stem, and those which tiller somewhat from the root, will suffer least under fly attack—the first, because the straw will not so readily bend or break at the point weakened by the maggot; and the second, because the flies of the second spring brood select fresh, young shoots for the deposition of their eggs in preference to the older and tougher stalks, with the effect to kill only these valueless sprouts, and to diminish by so much the injury to the heading stems.

Kansas Notes.—The Hessian Fly has been known in Kansas as a wheat pest since 1871. It is believed to have been imported into this country during the Revolutionary War, and since that time has been steadily gaining ground. In 1788 the wheat crop about Trenton, N. J., was a total failure because of the fly's work. In 1800 the pest did great damage in New York; in 1843 Maryland and Virginia were overrun. In 1844 it did much injury in northern Indiana and Illinois, and the contiguous portions of Michigan and Wisconsin. The following year it did more or less injury all over Illinois, and entered Georgia, where it worked great havoc in 1846.

The first serious invasion of Kansas occurred in 1884, although 1871, 1877 and 1880 were marked by its appearances. Concerning the 1884 invasion, Prof. F. H. Snow had to say, in the Fourth Biennial Report of the Kansas State Board of Agriculture (1883–'84), as follows (pages 604–606):

The most conspicuous entomological event of the year 1884 was the successful entrance within our borders of the far-famed Hessian Fly. This species appeared in such numbers as to properly entitle the movement to be called an invasion. The first mutterings of the invasion were heard in the month of May, from Wyandotte and Johnson counties, on the eastern border. In these counties it was reported that the "May" wheat was affected, and that the depredations were most extensive on lands cultivated in wheat the preceding year, and much worse on lands cultivated in wheat for three successive crops (M. B. Newman). Late in the autumn reports began to come in of a very general distribution of this army of invasion throughout the eastern third of the State. The weather of the year, while unfavorable for the Chinch-bug, was all that could be desired by the Hessian Fly, this species thriving in wet seasons, but languishing in dry seasons. Thus these two species seem to be each other's counterparts—bad weather for one being good weather for the other.

Direct reports have been received by the writer during the past two weeks from correspondents of the State Board of Agriculture in 35 different counties. Of these, 21 report the Hessian Fly as present to an extent varying from slight indications to very serious occupation. The western line of the invading army now rests between the 97th and 98th meridians, and the line is unbroken, from Sumner in the southern tier of counties, to Washington in the northern tier. This line passes through Sumner, Sedgwick, Harvey, Marion, Dickinson, and Clay, to Washington. No counties to the west of this line report the presence of the foe. No reports have been received from the southeastern counties excepting Cherokee, which reports a light attack of the fly. The other counties reporting its presence are Cowley, Morris, Davis, Riley, Pottawatomie, Wabaunsee, Shawnee, Douglas, Johnson, Wyandotte, Leavenworth, Atchison, Jackson, and Doniphan. Thus there is not only an unbroken line of the enemy from Sumner north to Washington, but also from Sumner northeast to Doniphan, in the northeastern corner of the State. The counties reporting the most serious injury are Doniphan, Atchison, Leavenworth, Wabaunsee, Davis, Riley, Morris, Dickinson, and Marion.

In 1885 the fly made a material spread within the State. In the monthly report of the Board of Agriculture for June, 1885, Professor Snow says:

An article detailing the life-history of this insect and suggesting remedies for its ravages was furnished by the writer in January last for the Fourth Biennial Report of the Kansas State Board of Agriculture. At that time the fly was reported to the writer from only 18 counties. At the present time it is reported from no fewer than 57 of the 81 organized counties of the State of Kansas. This increase in area of distribution is to be accounted for from the fact that the species is two-brooded, and that the second or spring brood made its presence felt in many counties in which the first brood was not sufficiently numerous to attract attention.

An analysis of the 57 counties reporting the Hessian Fly indicates that the wheat has been very seriously destroyed in 16 counties, moderately damaged in 11 counties, and but slightly injured in 30 counties. The 16 counties suffering serious damage are Atchison, Butler, Chase, Davis, Dickinson, Jackson, Labette, Leavenworth, Lincoln, Marion, Osborne, Ottawa, Rooks, Saline, Sedgwick, and Wabaunsee. The 11 counties sustaining a moderate loss are Cowley, Douglas, Doniphan, Harvey, Jefferson, Johnson, Linn, McPherson, Miami, Mitchell, and Osage. The 30 counties as yet but lightly afflicted are Allen, Brown, Chautauqua, Clay, Cloud, Coffey, Crawford, Elk, Ellis, Ellsworth, Franklin, Harper, Lyon, Marshall, Montgomery, Morris, Nemaha, Neosho, Norton, Reno, Riley, Rush, Russell, Shawnee, Smith, Sumner, Washington, Wilson, Woodson, and Wyandotte.

Since 1885 the Hessian Fly has remained "with us," doing annually considerable damage, though just how much it is difficult to estimate. The observations made on the fly in this State lead me to emphasize the previously-suggested remedy of *late planting*, at earliest after September 25, and the careful destruction of the early springing up volunteer wheat, as the two most beneficial measures to be adopted by the Kansas wheat-grower in his struggle with this pest.

WHEAT-STRAW WORM.

(*Isosoma tritici* Riley; Order, Hymenoptera.)

Diagnosis.—The plants stunted in growth; heads do not fill out, and ripen prematurely. Examination of the stem (by splitting it) shows one or more small, white grubs in the joints next to the head, or in the one next below this.

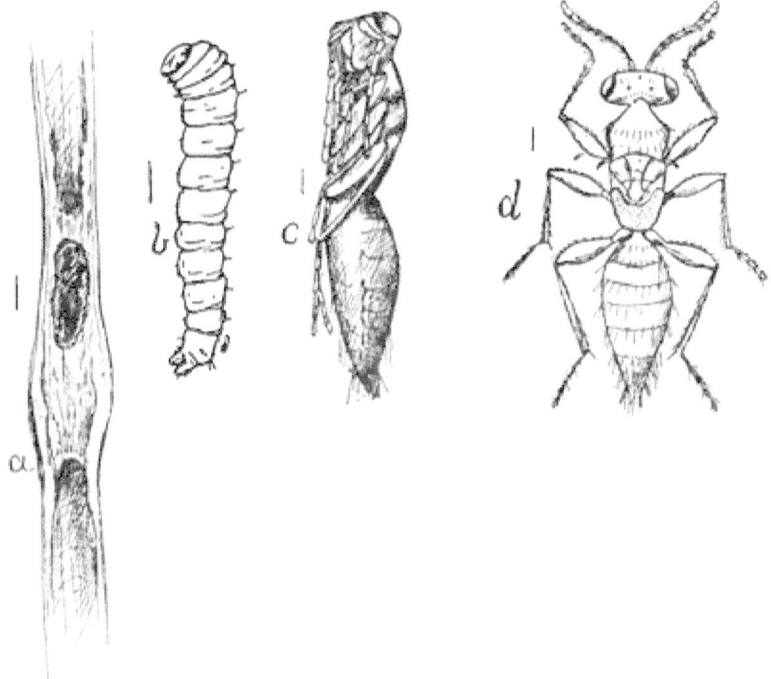

FIG. 17. WHEAT-STRAW WORM; *a*, pupa in cell in wheat straw; *b*, larva; *c*, pupa; *d*, adult (without wings).

Description and Life-history.—The adult insect is a very small, four-winged insect (most of the specimens are wingless), black, with green and blue metallic reflections. The damage to the wheat is done by the insect in its larval stage, when it appears as a small, white grub, less than one-fourth of an inch long, which lies in the heart of the stem near a joint. The grubs are provided with strong jaws, with which they gnaw the inner fiber of the stem, arresting a proper flow of the sap to the head. In March and April adults issue from last year's wheat straws (in the stack or in the stubble), and lay their eggs on the tender leaves of the growing wheat. The larvæ, on hatching, burrow into the stem, pupate, and soon mature, the adults emerging in the latter part of May and early part of June. These adults lay their eggs in the now ripening wheat, and another brood of destructive larvæ hatches. These larvæ pupate in the straws, either in stubble or stack, before winter, and pass the winter in the pupal stage. The following spring the adults appear, and a new cycle is begun. The insect is thus two-brooded.

Remedies.—The plainly-suggested remedy is to destroy the insect while hibernating in the pupal stage in the old straw. The stubble and all remnants of straw-stacks should be burned before March 1; that is, before the issuing of the adults in the spring. Whether the insect is present in the straw can be easily told during the winter, or by splitting open straws and examining. The pupæ, if present, will be found as small, dark, mummy-like objects, about one-fifth of an inch long, resting securely in small cells hollowed out in the center of the straw near a joint. As only about five out of every 100 individuals of this insect possess wings, the insect spreads very slowly from farm to farm, and, if all the hibernating individuals on a given farm be destroyed, there is no likelihood that the wheat on that farm can be attacked the following season.

This pest also suffers from the attacks of several parasitic insects, one of the most important of which, *Eupelmus allyni*, is a small, four-winged insect, which belongs to the same family as the pest itself. This *Eupelmus* parasite lays its eggs in the spring, after the Straw-worm larvæ have hatched, and the larvæ of the parasite, as soon as hatched, feed on the Straw-worm larvæ. By the middle of September the parasites have matured and escaped from the straws. Thus, the burning of the old straw in the winter not only kills the living Wheat-straw Worms which escaped the attacks of the parasites, but it does not destroy the helpful parasites.

Kansas Notes.—In 1885 Professor Snow reported this insect as inflicting serious depredations upon wheat in McPherson, Morris, Osborne, Ottawa and Saline counties. (Monthly Report Kansas Board of Agriculture for June, 1885.) The pest is spoken of in this report as a "new-comer to the State of Kansas." In a brief reference to the insect in the report of the Kansas Board of Agriculture for the quarter ending December 31, 1885, Professor Snow credits Warren Knaus, of McPherson, an entomologist of repute, with saying, "that according to his observation fully one-half of the larvæ and pupæ of this Wheat-worm have been destroyed by this parasite, a species of the genus *Pteromalus.*"

In a bulletin of this Department, issued in February, 1892, observations on the presence of this pest in Kansas in 1891 are presented. The insect was quite prevalent in central and western Kansas, Barton, Russell, Osborne, Rice, Ellsworth, Rush and Lincoln counties being especially infested.

Doubtless much damage is annually done to the wheat crop of Kansas by this insect; a considerable part of which damage is popularly accredited to the Hessian Fly.

WHEAT-HEAD ARMY-WORM.
(*Leucania albilinea* Guen; Order, Lepidoptera.)

Diagnosis.—The kernels of wheat are eaten out of the heads, leaving a head of chaff. The ground at the foot of the plants is frequently covered with chaff. A brown and pale-yellow caterpillar, about one inch long, feeding on the heads at night.

Description and Life-history.—The adult form of this insect is a yellowish and white moth, expanding about 1½ inches; front wings, pale straw; hind wings, satiny-white. The larva or caterpillar, in which form the insect commits its depredations, is, when full-grown, rather more than an inch in length; colors, pale yellow and brown; along the back there is a brown median line; on

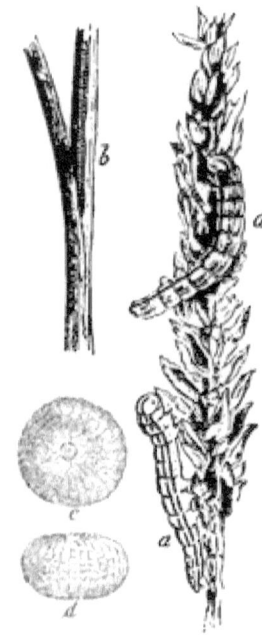

FIG. 18. WHEAT-HEAD ARMY-WORM; *a*, larvæ on wheat head; *b*, eggs between sheath and stalk; *c*, *d*, egg, top and side view, enlarged.

each side of this line, a narrow, sulphur-yellow stripe; still below, other brown and yellow lines. Below, dull white. Head large, pale yellow.

The first moths appear during May, in the latitude of St. Louis, according to Doctor Riley, and the bulk of the larvæ are full-grown about the time wheat is in the milk. The larvæ feed on the wheat heads until harvest, when they pupate, and the adult moths issue in the latter part of July. These lay eggs which produce a second brood of worms in August, the worms feeding on leaves. These larvæ pupate in September, and pass the winter as pupæ in the ground.

The feeding time of the larvæ when eating the wheat heads in June seems to be at night. A correspondent in Rush county writes:

The worms come up after dark, and feed upon the heads. They are in sufficient numbers to destroy the crop in some fields and parts of fields. Fields partly burned over have them only where fire did not run. Twelve acres isolated wheat on burnt stubble is free from them. Damage like the above is reported from all directions, but some wheat seems to be escaping everywhere. The best wheat is on ground fallow last year, and on which no wheat has been for several years.

Remedies.— No convenient effective remedy for the pest has yet been proposed. The remedies so far recognized are mostly preventive. The pupæ may be largely destroyed by late fall plowing and harrowing; and many moths may be captured in May by means of lights and sweetened and poisoned fluids. There are certain natural enemies; two parasitic Ichneumon flies and one Tachinid fly are noted by Doctor Riley. Kansas wheat-growers should give this pest special attention, to the end that a practical remedy for it may be found.

Kansas Notes.—Doctor Riley records the appearance of this insect in Dickinson, Douglas and Davis counties in 1876. (Ninth Annual Report State Entomologist of Missouri, p. 51.) The

Kansas Farmer of June 28, 1876, published several items indicating that the pest was occasioning some excitement in the State. Of 100 pupæ received by Doctor Riley from John Davis, of Junction City, 40 per cent. were infested by one of the parasitic Ichneumons.

From correspondents reporting in 1891, the presence of the worm was determined in several counties. A correspondent sending specimens June 13, from Stafford county, says: "They are doing an immense amount of damage to the wheat in this county."

FALL ARMY-WORM.

(*Laphygma frugiperda* Smith & Abb.)

Diagnosis.—A naked, pale-brown to dirty-green caterpillar, about one to one and a half inches long, eating grass, corn, rye, wheat, and various succulent plants in the autumn (September and October).

Description and Life-history—As an adult, this insect is a grayish-brown moth with an expanse of wings varying from one to one and a half inches; appearing in the fall. The larva or caterpillar, in which state the insect commits its depredations, is dark or even pitchy-black when young, but when full-grown is of a pale-brown or dirty-green color with more or less pink or yellow in the shape of fine mottlings. The body is longitudinally striped with dark lines. The head is pale yellowish with an inverted white, Y-shaped mark. The body is covered with many small, black tubercles, each tubercle bearing a short, stiff, black hair. The larvæ feed voraciously on all sorts of cereals and on many vegetables. They appear only in the fall, the first ones being seen about September 1, and the last ones about November 1,

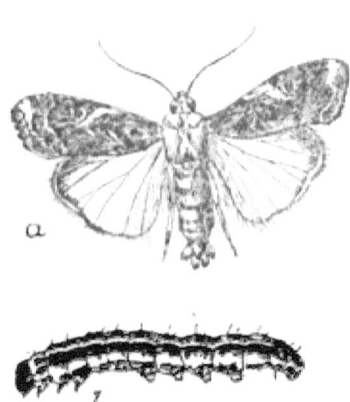

FIG. 19. FALL ARMY-WORM; *a*, adult; *b*, larva.

or a little later. There are at least two generations in a year. The eggs are deposited on the under sides of the leaves of peach, apple and other trees.

Remedies.—As the last brood of the year must pass the winter in the larval or pupal state in the ground, late fall plowing of fields in which the pest has been present during the fall will probably kill many. Also, if ground which is to be put into wheat be kept clean of vegetation before sowing, and the sowing be done late, the early moths will not be attracted to the field to lay their eggs. In Kansas in 1884, when the worm was numerous, many farmers in Douglas county waited until September 20 to October 20 before sowing their wheat and rye, and then had no trouble from the worm.

If these worms are invading a field of fall grain, most of them could be destroyed by running over them with a heavy roller without injury to the grain. Fortunately, wheat which is cut off by the worms is not necessarily destroyed. Several instances where a field was quite cut down, and yet where a good stand was got the following spring, are known.

Kansas Notes.—In a letter to the *Kansas Farmer* dated August 29, 1870, a correspondent in Mineral Point, Anderson county, calls attention to the presence of the pest, which is said to "take a 25-acre field in two days." This writer says that they last appeared in Kansas in 1866.

In the Fourth Biennial Report of the Kansas Board of Agriculture (1883–'84), Prof. F. H. Snow contributes some notes on this pest. It was present in considerable numbers in Douglas, Leavenworth, Jefferson and Labette counties. In Douglas county most of the damage was done during the first week in September. Wheat and rye sowed after September 15 was uninjured.

OTHER INSECTS ATTACKING WHEAT.

CHINCH-BUG.
ROCKY MOUNTAIN LOCUST.
INJURIOUS GRASSHOPPERS.

INSECTS ATTACKING OTHER CEREALS AND GRASSES.

INJURIOUS GRASSHOPPERS.
(Family *Acrididæ;* Order, Orthoptera.)

Diagnosis.— Grasshoppers of various species; attacking cereals and grass crops of all kinds.

Attacking, also, fruit- and shade-trees and garden crops.

Descriptions and Life-history.— The life-histories of the various injurious grasshoppers to be found in Kansas are so nearly parallel that a single, generalized life-history may be given which will practically serve for all.

The grasshopper or locust (I shall use these common names synonymously in this connection) has an incomplete metamorphosis (see p. 5), the young when hatched resembling the parents in form and habits. The striking difference between adult and newly-hatched young is the absence of wings in the infant, so that its only methods of locomotion are walking and hopping. The eggs are extruded by the female in masses, and deposited a short distance beneath the surface of the ground by means of the strong ovipositor. (See Fig. 13.) The eggs are deposited in the fall, and the young do not hatch until the following spring. The young are furnished with strong jaws, as the adults, and begin immediately to "make their own living." The increase in size stretches the chitinized and rather unyielding skin to bursting, and the first moult soon occurs. After this moult small wing-pads, the rudiments of the coming wings, are to be seen. With each successive moult the wing-pads are seen to be larger in size, until, at the last moult (the fourth, usually), they are fully developed, and the grasshopper is said to be full-grown, or adult. The time between hatching and maturity is between 70 and 100 days, varying in the different species. The following species do more or less damage annually in Kansas:

RED-LEGGED LOCUST (*Melanoplus femur-rubrum* De Geer).

This locust is a common native species, occurring all over the State. It is almost identical in size and appearance with the

Rocky Mountain Locust (*M. spretus* Thomas), being distinguished from it by the shorter forewings (never extending, when folded, beyond tip of abdomen) and the bluntly rounded and broadly notched, instead of the rather narrowly rounded and acutely notched (*spretus*) tip of the last abdominal segment of the male. (See Fig. 12.) Our native Red-leg is non-migratory, and, while appearing locally numerous, rarely does serious damage. It appears, winged, about the middle of August, or a little later. Doctor Riley has noted that the period between hatching and maturity, at St. Louis, is about 70 days.

DIFFERENTIAL LOCUST (*Melanoplus differentialis* Thomas).

This is one of the most common native locusts, and often does considerable local damage, especially in the southwestern part of the State. This locust is larger than *spretus* or *femur-rubrum*, being about 1½ inches long and its wings expanding 2½ inches, and is of a general bright yellowish-green color. "The head and thorax are olive-brown, and the front wings, very much of the same color and without other marks, have a brownish shade at base; the hind wings being tinged with green; the hind thighs are bright yellow, especially below, with the four black marks as in *spretus;* and the hind shanks are yellow with black spines, and a black ring near the base." This locust is partial to alfalfa and to various shade-trees.

FIG. 20. DIFFERENTIAL LOCUST.

TWO-STRIPED LOCUST (*Melanoplus bivittatus* Say).

This locust is of about the same size as *differentialis*, resembles it considerably, and is found in company with it. It is distinguished from *differentialis* "in having two lateral, yellowish stripes from the head to the extremities of the wing-covers." (See Figs. 22 and 23.) It is usually not so abundant as *differentialis*.

LONG-WINGED LOCUST (*Dissosteira longipennis* Thomas).

This locust, not until recently recognized as an injurious species, because of its comparative rarity, more nearly resembles the mi-

FIG. 21. LONG-WINGED LOCUST.

gratory locusts of the Old World than any other of our American forms. It is about two inches long from head to tip of folded wing-covers, and measures about 3½ inches from tip to tip of expanded wing-covers. The wing-covers or forewings are irregularly blotched with pale brown, and the hind wings are black, excepting the clear apical third and a narrow, clear, marginal border running back to the anal angles. This locust is a non-migratory form, occasionally abundant on the plains of eastern Colorado. It sometimes occurs in sufficient numbers in restricted areas to destroy all vegetation (see Kansas Notes).

Remedies.—The following notes on remedial measures are drawn from a pamphlet on "Destructive Locusts," by Dr. C. V.

Riley. (Bulletin 25, 1891, Division of Entomology, U. S. Department of Agriculture.)

The means to be employed (for the destruction of locusts) fall very naturally into five divisions: (1) Encouragement of natural agencies; (2) destruction of the eggs; (3) destruction of the young or unfledged insects; (4) destruction of the mature or winged insects; (5) preventive measures.

1. Under this head may come protection of the locust-eating birds, or, at least, non-destruction of them. Prairie chickens and quails do much good because of their grasshoper-eating habits.

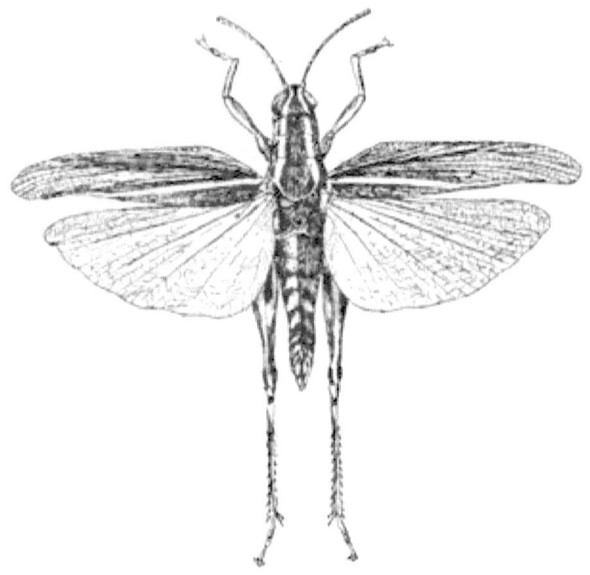

FIG. 22. TWO STRIPED LOCUST. (See page 42.)

There are many parasites of grasshoppers, but their control is outside of our hands. Certain minute mites and certain flies do most valiant work in the warfare against the locusts. A parasitic fungus growing in and on the bodies of the locusts sometimes destroys many.

2. Destruction of the eggs by harrowing or plowing, or tramping, or collecting, or flooding (in irrigated districts), in the fall is an effective measure. The ovipositing regions can be discovered by noting the dead bodies of locusts on the ground in autumn, or by turning over the ground here and there and exposing the eggs. The eggs of the Rocky Mountain Locust "are laid in bare, sandy places, especially on high, dry ground, which is tolerably compact

and not loose." Newly-plowed land is not liked. Moist or wet ground is generally avoided. Closely-grazed meadows and pastures are favorite egg-laying ground. The eggs of the Rocky Mountain Locust cannot be found in Kansas, except in the fall following an invasion by adults from the northwest.

The Red-legged, the Differential and the Two-striped locusts have about the same egg-laying habits as the Rocky Mountain Locust. The Differential occasionally deposits its eggs "under the bark of logs that have been felled on low land."

3. Destruction of the young or unfledged locusts in the spring may be accomplished in a number of ways. The young locusts, being wingless, are restricted in their range, are confined to the ground, and are usually thickly massed. *Burning*, by scattering old straw or hay over the infested areas and lighting it; or by means of machines, consisting of long, open grates with screens above directing the heat down, and drawn by horses over the fields; or by dragging a long wire, wrapped in rags which have been soaked in kerosene and ignited, back and forth over the field, is effective. *Crushing*, where the locusts are on hard, smooth ground, by heavy rollers, can be often indulged in. *Trapping* or *catching*, by the use of nets, or by ditches or trenches, or by machines, into which the locusts are fanned or sucked, and dropped into kerosene, is sometimes feasible. *Poisoning* may be effectively used when it is desired to protect a certain limited area, or special crops, fruit- or shade-trees, etc. Paris green, mixed with 20 to 30 parts of flour, and scattered on the ground, destroys many locusts attracted by the flour. Spraying trees, bushes or garden crops with Paris green (see p. 7) can be relied on.

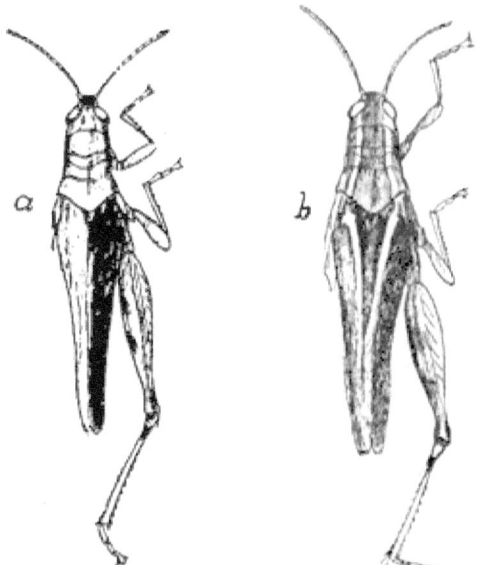

FIG. 23. *a*, DIFFERENTIAL LOCUST; *b*, TWO-STRIPED LOCUST; to show difference in markings, when wings are folded. (See page 42.)

The protection of fruit- or shade-trees against the young Differential and Two-striped locusts can usually be effectively done. Doctor Riley's recommendations are as follows:

> Where the trunks are smooth and perpendicular they may be protected by whitewashing. The lime crumbles under the feet of the insects as they attempt to climb, and prevents their getting up. By their persistent efforts, however, they gradually wear off the lime and reach a higher point each day, so that the whitewashing must be often repeated. Trees with short, rough trunks, or which lean, are not well protected in this way. A strip of smooth, bright tin answers even better for the same purpose. A strip three or four inches wide, brought around and tacked to a smooth tree, will protect it, while on rougher trees a piece of old rope may first be tacked around the tree and the tin tacked to it, so as to leave a portion both above and below. Passages between the tin and rope or the rope and tree can then be blocked by filling the upper area between the tin and tree with earth. The tin must be high enough from the ground to prevent the 'hoppers from jumping from the latter beyond it, and the trunk below the tin, where the insects collect, should be covered with some coal-tar or poisonous substance to prevent girdling. This is more especially necessary with small trees, and coal-tar will answer as such preventive.
>
> One of the cheapest and simplest modes is to encircle the tree with cotton batting, in which the insects will entangle their feet and thus be more or less obstructed. Strips of paper covered with tar, stiff paper tied on so as to slope, roof-fashion, strips of glazed wall-paper, and thick coatings of soft soap, have been used with varying success; but no estoppel equals the tight tin. The others require constant watching and removal, and in all cases coming under our observation some insects would get into the trees, so as to require the daily shaking of these morning and evening. This will sometimes have to be done when the bulk of the insects have become fledged, even when tin is used, for a certain proportion of the insects will then fly into the trees. They do most damage during the night, and care should be had that the trees be unloaded of their voracious freight just before dark.

Mr. George Gibbs, of Holden, Missouri, found that the whitewash was rendered still more effectual by adding one-half pint of turpentine to the pailful.

4. The complete destruction of the winged insects, when they swoop down upon a country in prodigious swarms, is impossible. Man is powerless before the mighty host. Special plants or small tracts of vegetation may be saved by perseveringly driving the insects off, or keeping them off by means of smudges, as the locusts avoid smoke.

Certain of the means used in fighting young locusts (unfledged ones) are available to some extent in the warfare against the winged ones. In the morning and evening, when they are little inclined to take wing, the various methods of catching and crushing may be used.

Kansas Notes.—The Red-legged Locust (*Melanoplus femur-rubrum*) has not been known, in recent years at least, to do serious damage in the State, even locally. It may be seen, however, every summer in comparative abundance on the road-side plants and among rank vegetation.

The Differential Locust (*Melanoplus differentialis*) has, annually, of late, committed depredations of some extent in the western, especially southwestern, part of the State. Last year (1891), reports from Garden City (Finney county) during the latter half of July indicated the presence of *differentialis* and *bivittatus* in alarming numbers in growing crops, especially alfalfa. This year, Hamilton county has reported (V. S. Jones, Syracuse, July 28) *differentialis* and *bivittatus*. "They are eating nearly everything bearing fruit," writes Mr. Jones. "I think they are worse on mulberry and catalpa trees."

In the fall of 1891, Prof. Herbert Osborn, special agent of the Division of Entomology, United States Department of Agriculture, visited Kansas to investigate the reported damages by grasshoppers. His report is published in Bulletin No. 27 (1892) of the division. Professor Osborn found *differentialis* and *bivittatus* in Finney county seriously injuring the alfalfa. He says:

> The alfalfa was badly stripped, the blossoms and seeds entirely eaten up, and in many patches the stems were stripped bare of leaves, looking brown and dead. The grasshoppers, mostly *differentialis*, with a considerable number of *bivittatus*, when rising in front of me as I walked through the field, formed a cloud 8 or 10 feet high, and so dense as to hide objects beyond them. The territory examined was the irrigated portion of the Arkansas valley, lying in Finney, Kearny and Hamilton counties. . . . The whole area extends, with occasional breaks, a distance of about 50 miles along the river, and forms a strip from one to five miles wide, but limited entirely to areas where irrigation has been practiced.

According to Professor Osborn, "alfalfa is the crop in which there is the most loss, but orchards are [were] suffering badly, and, were they extensive throughout the district, would very probably present the heavier loss." Professor Osborn believes that the eggs are deposited along the sides of or in the irrigating ditches, which are dry during a large part of the year. On this belief (which seems to be founded on sufficient evidence) he makes the following recommendations for fighting the pests:

1. To thoroughly break up the surface of the ground in and along the ditches before winter by harrowing thoroughly, cultivating or shallow plowing, thus exposing the eggs to winter weather and natural enemies.

2. Wherever practicable, to flood the ground for a day or two at the time young locusts are hatching. I was told that the young 'hoppers were entirely unaffected by water, as they would crawl up the alfalfa stems and escape, and it is probable that sufficient flooding to accomplish much good in this region is out of the question. My only hope in this line would be in watching carefully for the time of hatching, and using the water before the 'hoppers had obtained any growth; and, if abundant along the ditches, putting a little kerosene on the water.

3. A use of the *hopper-dozer as early in the season as possible, when I believe the treatment of a strip 8 or 10 feet wide on each side of the ditches would destroy so large a part of their numbers as to prevent any serious damage. As I learned from a number of parties the 'hoppers are scarcely half-grown when the crop is cut, it would seem that immediately after cutting the first crop would be the best time to use the hopper-dozer. The 'hoppers would be large enough to jump readily, and the dozers could be run very easily. It would be difficult to use them at any other time than directly after the crop was cut, as the dense growth of alfalfa would obstruct their movement.

My strongest recommendation would be the urging of effort in breaking up egg masses before winter, and then, in case locusts still appear in any number in spring, to resort to the dozers at first opportunity. I believe active use of these measures will be effectual, with a cost but trifling compared with the value of the crop to be saved.

Skunks, toads and certain Tachinid flies do much toward keeping these pests in check. Professor Osborn states that he noted several dead grasshoppers which "had the appearance of having been affected with *Entomophthora*."

I attempted last summer (1891) to inoculate specimens of *differentialis* and *bivittatus* from Garden City with *Empusa (Entomophthora?) aphidis,* (a parasitic fungus growing freely on Chinch-bugs in our laboratories,) by enclosing the grasshoppers

---

*A "hopper-dozer" is a machine for catching grasshoppers, usually in the nature of a broad tray containing coal-tar or kerosene, to be pushed or pulled over the infested field. The grasshoppers fly or hop into the tray, or are sucked in by means of fans, and meet a sticky or oily death in the tray. (For descriptions and directions for construction of "hopper-dozers" or locust-catchers, see "Destructive Locusts:" Riley, Bulletin 23 (1891), Division of Entomology, U. S. Department of Agriculture.)

with Chinch-bugs dead and dying from the effects of the growth of the fungus. I was unsuccessful.

The Long-winged Locust (*Dissosteira longipennis*), while doing much damage in a restricted portion of eastern Colorado (400 square miles) last year, has not yet appeared in Kansas in serious numbers. Professor Osborn found it "at all points visited in Finney, Kearny, Hamilton and Greeley counties;" but "at no point did it occur in destructive numbers, and I should not look for any injury from it in these localities in the near future, at least," says this competent entomologist.

OTHER INSECTS ATTACKING CEREALS (BESIDES CORN AND WHEAT) AND GRASSES.

CHINCH-BUG.
SOUTHERN CORN-ROOT WORM.
ROCKY MOUNTAIN LOCUST.
GARDEN WEB-WORM.
FALL ARMY-WORM.
INJURIOUS GRASSHOPPERS.

STORED-GRAIN INSECTS.

ANGOUMOIS GRAIN MOTH.
(*Gelechia cereallella* Oliv.; Order, Lepidoptera.)

Diagnosis.—Kernels of corn shelled or in the ear, grains of wheat, etc., showing a small, round hole; when a handful of the grain is thrown into water, some of the kernels (the attacked ones) float.

Description and Life-history.—The adult form of the insect is a small moth about one-fourth of an inch in length, and about one-half an inch from tip to tip of expanded wings. As a larva or grub, during which stage the damage is done, it is found burrowing within kernels of various stored grains, eating out the inside starchy portion, and leaving only a shell.

The moths fly about at night, and lay their eggs either on standing grain in the field or on stored grain in bins and cribs. There are probably four or five broods each year in this State. The eggs are deposited at the base of the kernel, so that the larva or grub on hatching makes its entrance hole at the base. This hole is usually filled with excreta, so that it is not noticeable. The larva after some time changes into a quiescent pupa. Just before this

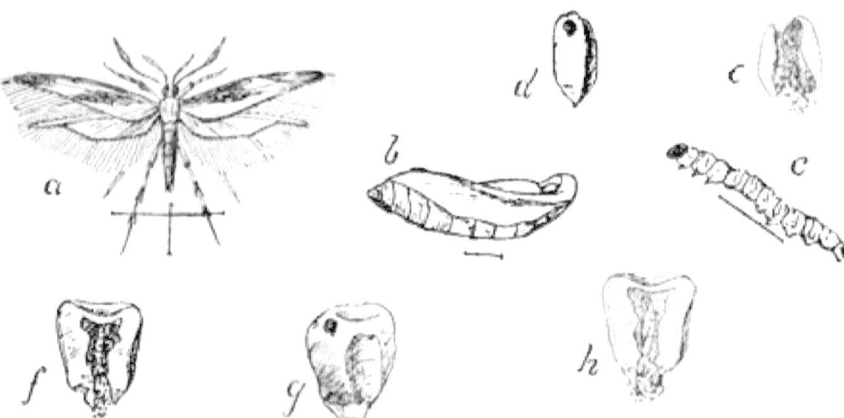

FIG. 24. ANGOUMOIS GRAIN MOTH; *a*, adult; *b*, pupa; *c*, larva; *d*, infested wheat grain, outside appearance; *e*, wheat grain, opened, with larva within; *f*, section of kernel of corn, showing larva; *g*, infested kernel of corn, outside appearance; *h*, section of kernel of corn, showing pupa.

change, a hole is gnawed by the larva at the apex of the kernel for the exit of the future moth. This hole is conspicuous, and is the one referred to in the diagnosis as betraying infested grains.

Kernels of suspected grain should be split open; if infested by the pest, either a small, white, brown-headed grub, with nine pairs of legs, or a brown, mummy-like pupa, with wing-pads, antennæ, and legs closely pressed against the body, will be seen. Or there may be found the perfect moth, with folded wings, ready to emerge from the kernel.

Remedies.— Fortunately effective remedies are at hand for the attacks of these stored-grain pests. In 1879 Dr. C. V. Riley called attention to the use of bi-sulphide of carbon, on a large scale, as an insecticide, and this substance may be effectually used against the Grain Moth. Bi-sulphide of carbon is sold at retail by druggists for about 25 cents a pound, but it may be bought for considerably less when got in larger quantities. It is an extremely volatile liquid, and the insects are killed by its vapor. It is necessary, therefore, that it be so applied that the vapor may penetrate all through the bin of grain.

The grain to be treated should be in a tight bin. If the grain is not stored in tight bins, such a bin, or box, should be constructed, and the grain treated in it in successive portions. If the grain is wheat or oats or shelled corn, a long tube, open at both ends, but carrying within it a snugly-fitting rod, should be thrust into the grain until one end of the tube is near the center of the bin. The rod should now be withdrawn, and a quantity of the bi-sulphide of carbon should be poured into the tube. About one ounce of liquid to each 100 pounds of grain in the bin should be used. Finally, the tube should be withdrawn, the liquid being left in the center of the grain mass.

Another recommended method of applying the insecticide is that of soaking with it a ball of cotton fastened to the end of a pole. The soaked cotton may now be pushed into the grain. Two or three applications of this kind, in different places in the bin, will effectually destroy all insect life in the bin. If the corn is in the ear, a convenient method of application is to pour the bi-sulphide of carbon into small, open dishes, setting these dishes about on the corn; or, the surface of the stored corn may be sprinkled with the liquid. The fumes of the bi-sulphide are heavier than air, so that they sink down into the bin. *Great* care must be taken that no lighted lamps, cigars or burning material shall come near the bi-sulphide of carbon, or near places where it has been used, until the odor has passed entirely away. The liquid is highly inflammable and explosive. No danger, however, need exist if proper care be taken. Grain treated with bi-sulphide of carbon is not injured at all by the insecticide. The bad odor passes off in a few days.

Kansas Notes.—In a bulletin issued by this Department in February, 1892, attention is called to the occurrence of this pest in Kansas. At this writing (October, 1892), this insect is threatening to injure the cereal specimens collected by the State for exhibit at the World's Fair. The specimens are stored in a large warehouse at Topeka, in which the moths are abundant. The pest does great damage in the Southern States, where as many as eight generations are produced in a year.

GRAIN WEEVILS.

(*Calandria* species; Order, Coleoptera.)

Diagnosis.—About same as for Grain Moth. A footless grub; pupa without long feelers, or adult beetle, instead of moth will be found within the kernels.

Description and Life-history.—The adult insect is a small, dark-colored snout-beetle, which lays its eggs on the grain. The small, footless larvæ soon hatch and eat their way into the kernels, maturing in a few weeks. There are several broods each year. Corn, oats, wheat, barley and other stored grains are indiscriminately attacked.

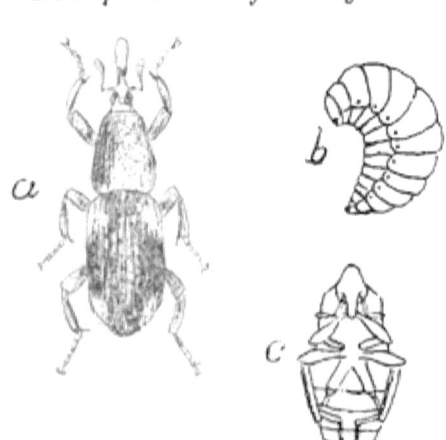

FIG. 25. GRAIN WEEVIL: *a*, adult; *b*, larva; *c*, pupa, all enlarged.

Remedies.—Same as for Grain Moth.

Kansas Notes.—These weevils have been known to do considerable damage in Lawrence mills.

FLAX-SEED MITE.
(*Tyroglyphus* sp.; Order, Acarina.)

Diagnosis.—An increasing quantity of fine debris or dust in the bin or box containing the flax-seed. On close examination, many microscopic, whitish, moving insects.

Description and Life-history.—This flax-seed-eating mite closely resembles the common flour and cheese mite, but is probably a different species. Mites may be distinguished from other minute insects by their having four pairs of legs instead of three, as with true insects. The Flax-seed Mite is white and soft, and is so small that many of them together resemble fine, white dust. They occasionally occur in immense numbers in bins of flax-seed in warehouses or elevators. One correspondent reports them as several inches deep on the floor of an old bin. In the infested bins there will be seen a quantity of brown, earthy-looking substance, which is composed of the body remnants of the mites. It is probable that the mites attack only broken or partially decaying seeds.

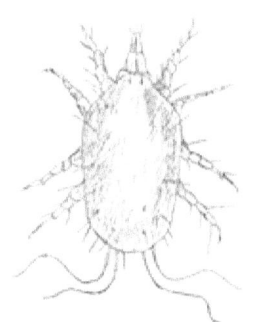

FIG. 26. FLAX-SEED MITE, greatly enlarged.

Remedies.—There is to be found almost always associated with this Flax-seed Mite another slightly larger mite (*Cheyletus* sp.) which preys upon it, and does much to reduce the numbers of the pest. If these other mites are present, they will probably succeed in practically exterminating the Flax-seed Mite in the course of a few weeks.

The burning of sulphur in the infested building is recommended. If the mites are confined to one or two bins, bi-sulphide of carbon should be introduced, as recommended in case of Angoumois Grain Moth (p. 50), remembering the highly inflammable nature of the substance.

If the elevator or grain building is thoroughly infested with the mites, only the most radical measures will rid it of the pests. The contents should be removed, so far as possible, and the building thoroughly dried and fumigated.

Kansas Notes.—Miss Mary Murtfeldt, of Missouri, in a note in Insect Life, (vol. II, p. 251, January and February, 1890,) mentions the occurrence of the Flax-seed Mite in a warehouse at Paola. Some 4,000 bushels of stored flax-seed were infested, and the mites were present in such amazing numbers that the owner feared they would destroy the entire stock.

At the twenty-third annual meeting of the Kansas Academy of Science, Lawrence, November, 1890, Prof. D. S. Kelly, of the State Normal School, Emporia, exhibited specimens of the mites and injured flax-seed taken at Emporia.

Several occurrences of the mite in the State have been reported to this Department.

INSECTS ATTACKING GARDEN VEGETABLES.

TORTOISE BEETLES.

(Species of *Cassida* and *Coptocycla;* Order. Coleoptera.)

Diagnosis.—Attacking sweet-potatoes; small, turtle-shaped beetles, some of them with bright, metallic tints, feeding on the leaves; or the larvæ (young) of these beetles, in general shape like the beetles, broad and flattened, but the margin of the body armed with spines, feeding on the leaves.

Description and Life-history.—There are a half-dozen species of these Tortoise Beetles, belonging to the genera *Cassida* and

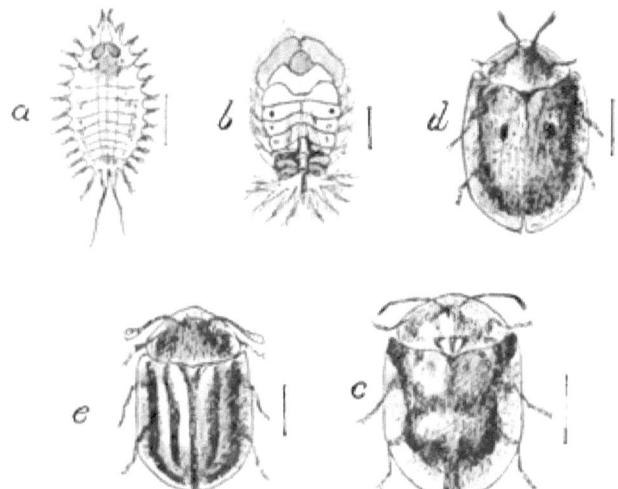

FIG. 27. TORTOISE BEETLES; *a*, larva of Mottled Tortoise Beetle (*Coptocycla guttata* Oliv.); *b*, pupa of same; *c*, adult of same; *d*, adult Black-legged Tortoise Beetle (*Cassida nigripes* Oliv.); *e*, adult Two-striped Tortoise Beetle (*Cassida bivittata* Say).

Coptocycla, which attack the sweet-potato. There are hardly any other insects which infest this plant, but these beetles are often sufficient in number to do great injury.

The larvæ of all resemble each other in being short, broad, and flattened; in having six short, thick, fleshy legs, besides a movable, forked tail; and in having the margin of the body provided with spines.

The beetles are rather oval in form, flattened, and spread out like the shell of a turtle. This turtle-like effect is heightened by the peculiar markings of the back, the dark center often showing two or four foot-like dark projections pushing out to the rim of the shell. One species is of the most beautiful golden color when alive; another is pale yellow, striped with black.

The eggs of these beetles are deposited singly on the leaves. The larvæ and the adult beetles usually remain on the under side of the leaves, gnawing irregular holes in them. They are most abundant during May and June, and have an especial fondness for the young plants.

Remedies.—Paris green, one part of the poison to two parts of flour, sprinkled on the ground under the vines will kill the insects.

Paris green or London purple, one pound to 100 gallons of water (see p. 7), may be sprayed on the plants with good effect. If the under side of the leaves can be sprayed it is better. However, as the insects eat the entire leaf, spraying from above will answer. The spraying should be done as soon as the plants are well rooted, and two applications, with an interval of a week, should be sufficient.

It is highly advisable to keep a close watch on the young plants (examining the under sides of the leaves) and to pick off by hand any larvæ or beetles found. There are probably several generations of the pest in the year, and if many of the first ones to appear are destroyed there will be a large reduction of the possible numbers in succeeding generations during the season.

Kansas Notes.—These pests occasionally seriously injure the sweet-potato crop in the State.

SQUASH BUG.

(*Anasa tristis* De Geer; Order, Hemiptera.)

Diagnosis.—Infesting the squash; a rather large, flattened, rusty-black, ill-smelling bug, about one-half an inch long, with a pointed, sucking beak, attacking the leaves; the leaves become yellow and sickly; if the bugs are numerous, attacked plants may die.

Description and Life-history.—The adult is a familiar insect. Its large size and disgusting odor make it conspicuous. It is rusty black above and ochre-yellow beneath. It passes the winter in the adult stage under boards, logs, or other covering. It does not appear in the squash patch until late in the spring, often not until June or July. The eggs are laid on the under sides of the squash leaves in small patches. The young bugs when first hatched have a green body, with head, thorax and antennæ pink. Two days after hatching, the body becomes ash-gray, and the other portions black. The young begin to suck the juices from the leaves, and the plant becomes sickly.

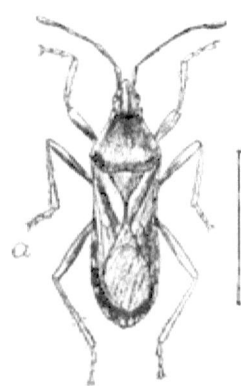

FIG. 28. SQUASH-BUG.

Remedies.—Hand-picking when the adult bugs first appear in June, before the eggs are laid; crushing the eggs found on the under sides of the leaves; picking off the young, which when first hatched feed together in bunches; and trapping the bugs by laying pieces of board on the ground near the hills and examining the under sides of them morning and evening, are the most effective remedies. Trimming off the lower leaves of the plants, and laying them on the ground by the hills in place of the boards, is recommended. Kerosene emulsion (see page 9) has been used with good effect on the young bugs. Fertilizing helps the plants to withstand injury.

Kansas Notes.—A correspondent in La Blanche, Sherman county, reported (June 5, 1891) that he had grown squashes for seed for four years and that his vines were first attacked in 1890. The bugs did not appear until July. In 1891 they appeared in May, and did much injury.

HARLEQUIN CABBAGE BUG.
(*Murgantia histrionica* Hahn; Order, Hemiptera.)

Diagnosis.—Infesting cabbage, turnips, horse-radish, mustard, etc.; a flattened, oval bug about three-eighths of an inch long, with prominent black and orange-red markings, sucking the juices from the leaves; the attacked leaves look as if blistered, and entire leaves are often withered.

Description and Life-history.—The adult insect, which is a true sucking bug, is about three-eighths of an inch long and about one-fourth of an inch wide, flattened oval, tapering behind the middle to a rounded point. Above black, with orange-red spots and dashes; below black, with five longitudinal rows of orange-red spots. The young bugs are broadly oval and with slightly different markings.

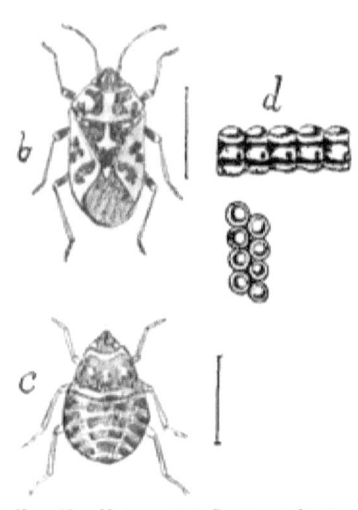

FIG. 29. HARLEQUIN CABBAGE BUG: b, adult; c, young; d, eggs.

The eggs are laid in March by adults which have passed through the winter. The eggs are usually 10 or 12 in number, and are laid in two rows, on the under sides of the leaves. The young are hatched in about a week, and immediately begin their destructive work by piercing the leaves and sucking the sap from them. The punctured leaves soon wilt and die. It is said that half a dozen adult insects will kill a cabbage in one day.

Remedies.—As the insects suck the juices from the leaves, instead of eating the soft leaf tissue, spraying arsenical poisons on the surface of the leaves will be ineffectual. Hot water, kerosene emulsion (see p. 9) and pyrethrum (see p. 9) are recommended. The bugs may be trapped, as recommended for Squash-bugs, by laying boards or leaves near the hills, under which the insects will congregate. High cultivation will enable the plants to resist the attacks of the pest.

Kansas Notes.—The insect is a native of the Gulf States and Mexico, Texas seeming to be the place of its greatest abundance. It has been making its way north since the close of the war. It was found in Missouri in 1870, and is said by Le Baron, in his sixth annual report as State Entomologist of Illinois, to have reached Kansas. This report was published in 1877.

In the Third Biennial Report of the Kansas State Board of Agriculture, 1881–'82, Prof. E. A. Popenoe says:

In the last few years it has been extending its range northward through Kansas, until now it appears to have spread over the greater part of the State.

In the Report of the Kansas State Horticultural Society for 1882, Mr. A. N. Godfrey reports that the pest appeared about the last week in July (1882) in Greenwood county in great numbers. It was found on cabbage, turnips, horse-radish, and mustard. He declares that it is generally considered a new insect among the farmers. In recent years it appears to have done little injury in the State.

IMPORTED CABBAGE-WORM.
(*Pieris rapæ* Linn.; Order, Lepidoptera.)

Diagnosis.—Infesting cabbage; a naked, green caterpillar about 1½ inches long, with a yellowish stripe along the back and a row of yellow spots along each side, and dotted all over with black, feeding on the leaves.

Description and Life-history.—The adult insect is a common white butterfly, the female having two black spots on each fore wing, while the male has but one black spot on each fore wing. The wings expand about 1¾ inches. The eggs are laid singly or in groups of two or three each on the young cabbage leaves; the larvæ, soon hatched, feed on the foliage and become full-grown in about two weeks. Changing to chrysalids, they remain in this quiescent stage for about 10 days, when the butterflies emerge and lay eggs for another brood of worms. There are several generations each season. The insect passes the winter in the chrysalid stage.

FIG. 30. IMPORTED CABBAGE-WORM; *a*, adult; *b*, larva.

Remedies.—When the worms appear in great numbers they are often entirely swept away in a given region by the spread of a contagious bacterial disease. Prof. S. A. Forbes has observed the workings of this disease in Illinois. In the fall of 1883, he found this disease to be raging among the cabbage-worms all over Illinois, and declares it to be his opinion that there are good grounds for belief that a means of successfully combatting the Cabbage-worm will be found in artificially spreading this contagious disease.

Searching for the eggs on the leaves and destroying them may be resorted to with advantage.

Pyrethum (see page 9) may be mixed with six to eight times its bulk of flour and dusted on the cabbage with a powder gun. This substance is not poisonous to human beings. It should be applied about once a week as long as any worms remain.

Dr. Riley advocates the use of hot water. He says:

> Every visible worm upon the cabbages may be killed by the use of water at the temperature of 130° Fahrenheit. The water may be boiling hot when put into the watering can, but it will not be too hot when it reaches the cabbage leaves.

Kansas Notes.—The Imported Cabbage-worm Butterfly is, as its name indicates, not a native of North America. It was introduced about 1856 or 1857, having been first taken at Quebec in 1859. In 1864 it had not extended more than forty miles from Quebec as a center. In 1866 it was taken in the northern part of New Hampshire and Vermont. It steadily spread north and west over the United States, until in 1880 it was found abundantly in eastern Kansas by Professor Snow.

SOUTHERN CABBAGE-WORM.
(*Pieris protodice* Boisd.; Order, Lepidoptera.)

Diagnosis.—Infesting cabbage; a black-dotted, greenish-blue caterpillar, with four longitudinal yellow stripes, feeding on the leaves.

Description and Life-history.—The adult is a butterfly of the same genus as the Imported Cabbage-worm Butterfly (*Pieris*). The black markings on the wings are more numerous and exten-

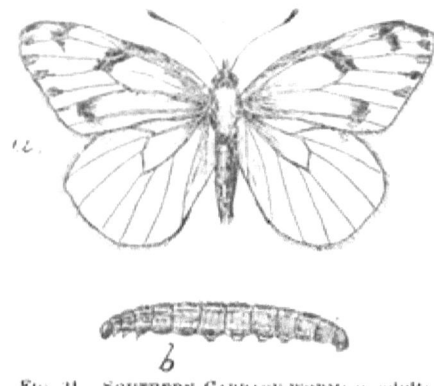

Fig. 31. SOUTHERN CABBAGE-WORM; a, adult; b, larva.

sive than in *rapæ*. The female *protodice* is altogether darker than the male. The insect is two-brooded, second brood hibernating in the chrysalid stage.

Remedies.—As for Imported Cabbage-worms.

Kansas Notes.—This cabbage pest is not as injurious as the Imported Cabbage-worm, or the Cabbage Plusia.

CABBAGE PLUSIA.

(*Plusia brassicæ* Riley; Order, Lepidoptera.)

Diagnosis.—Infesting cabbage, turnip, tomato, celery, clover, etc.; caterpillars about one inch long, pale green, with paler longitudinal lines, eating large, irregular holes in the leaves; the caterpillars have but five pairs of legs instead of eight pairs, as is the case with the Imported Cabbage-worms, and loop the body when walking, like a span worm.

Description and Life-history.—The adult is a moth, expanding about 1½ inches, smoky gray with brownish tinge, and marked in the middle of each front wing with a small, silvery, V-shaped mark and a small, oval dot. The moth flies at night. The eggs are laid on the cabbage leaves, and as soon as hatched the young larvæ begin to feed on their favorite food-plant. The larva, (described in the diagnosis,) when full-grown, spins a thin, loose, white cocoon, often between the cabbage leaves, and pu-

Fig. 32. CABBAGE PLUSIA; a, adult; b, larva.

pates. The moth soon emerges and lays eggs for another generation. The larvæ are to be noticed especially in August and September.

Remedies.—The same remedies recommended for the Imported Cabbage-worms are applicable to the Cabbage Plusia.

Kansas Notes.—This pest at times does much damage to cabbages in Douglas county.

PEA WEEVIL.

(*Bruchus pisi* Linn.; Order. Coleoptera.)

Diagnosis.—Many small, grayish, snouted beetles (the adult weevils) among stored peas in winter and spring; many of the peas with small, circular holes. The weeviled peas will float in water.

Description and Life-history.—The adult is a beetle about one-fifth of an inch long; general color rusty or grayish-black, with a small, white spot on the thorax. The eggs are laid on the green, young pea pods in the summer. The eggs are small, fusiform, and yellow. The grubs on hatching bore through the pod into the peas. The hole made in the growing pea soon closes up, leaving the voracious larva within. If the pea is used for food the larva comes to an untimely end, being fairly "in the soup," so to speak. If the peas are allowed to ripen and put away for seed, the larva continues its eating until there is only a shell left of the pea. Weeviled peas are unfit for food, and, as proved by the experiments of Professor Popenoe, should not be used for seed. During the fall and winter the larvæ pupate and finally mature as weevils (the adult beetles). Some of the beetles emerge from the peas, while others remain in them until they are planted.

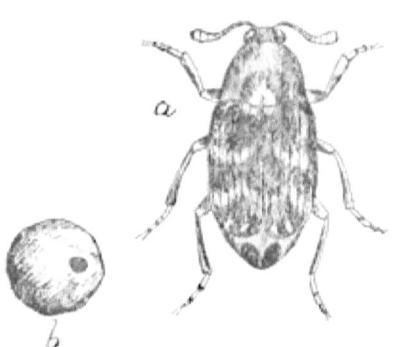

FIG. 33. PEA WEEVIL: *a*, adult; *b*, infested pea. Enlarged.

Remedies.—Infested peas should be put into an air-tight box or bin and treated with bi-sulphide of carbon (see p. 10). This fluid is poisonous and inflammable, and must be handled with great care. Its fumes are heavier than air, so that the liquid may be sprinkled over the surface of the peas, or put into an open dish resting on the peas.

Immersing the infested peas for a minute or two in water heated to 140° Fahrenheit will kill all contained weevils and larvæ.

Kansas Notes.—This insect is commonly injurious all over the State.

BEAN WEEVIL.
(*Bruchus obtectus* Say: Order, Coleoptera.)

Diagnosis.—Stored beans with a number of small, circular holes, or dark, discolored, circular spots; small weevils (beetles) crawling among the beans.

Description and Life-history.—The adult Bean Weevil much resembles the Pea Weevil, but is little more than one-half as large. It is dark colored, lacking the white spot on the thorax. The life-history is about the same as that of the Pea Weevil, the eggs being laid on the young bean pods, of course, instead of the pea pods. In the case of the Pea Weevil but one larva enters a pea, while with the Bean Weevil several larvæ may find homes in a single bean. When the stored beans are white, the presence of the weevil is easily detected by the dark eye-spot which lies over the cell of one of the enclosed larvæ. The spot is caused by the fact

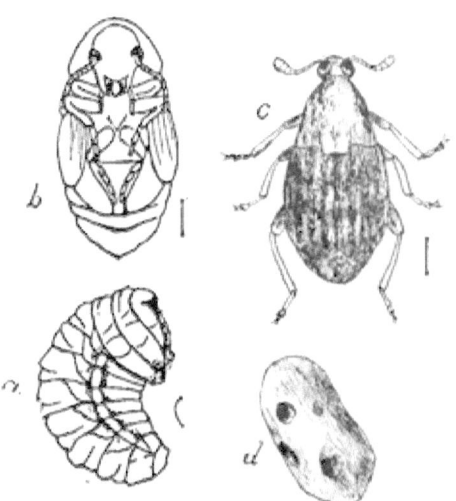

FIG. 34. BEAN WEEVIL; *a*, larva; *b*, pupa; *c*, adult; *d*, infested bean.

that at this point only a very thin membrane has been left by the larva, through which the adult beetle is to make its way into the outer world. Showing through the membrane is the dark, excrementitious matter filling up the cell. If the beans are dark, these spots do not show so plainly.

Remedies.—Same as for Pea Weevil.

Kansas Notes.—Prof. E. A. Popenoe gave this pest attention in the Second Annual Report of the Experiment Station, Kansas Agricultural College, for the year 1889 (p. 206 *et seq.*) He states that Limas, English beans and the French asparagus bean are practically exempt from attack, as far as his observation goes; in a few cases weevils were found to have developed in the large white Limas. Professor Popenoe's observations on the germinating power of the weeviled beans contradict the statements of earlier writers, notably Dr. Riley,[*] in that 47 per cent. of the weeviled beans coming under Professor Popenoe's observation in the summer of 1889 were without germinating power, the plumule, radicle, and cotyledons, constituting the resting germ of the bean, all suffering from the attack of the weevil. Professor Popenoe recommends killing the weevils when the beans are first stored, as it is evident that the beetles continue to breed and develop in the dry, stored beans, thus increasing in numbers and in destructive effect.

TOMATO-WORM.

(*Phlegethontius carolina*, Linn.; Order, Coleoptera.)

Diagnosis.—Infesting tomatoes; a large, "ugly," green worm (when full-grown three inches long), with several oblique, whitish stripes on each side of the body and a prominent "horn" on the tail, feeding on the leaves. Sometimes the worms are brown instead of green.

Description and Life-history.—The adult is a large, gray "hawk-moth," with orange-colored spots along each side of the abdomen. The moth has an expanse of wings of four or five inches. The

---

[*] Dr. Riley, in Insect Life, vol. IV, p. 297, (June, 1892,) refers to Professor Popenoe's experiments, saying that it is evident that weeviled peas and beans are unfit for seed.

eggs are laid in the evening, on tomato plants; the larvæ feed voraciously for about three weeks, when they go into the ground and pupate. The chrysalis is a peculiar object, being a rather

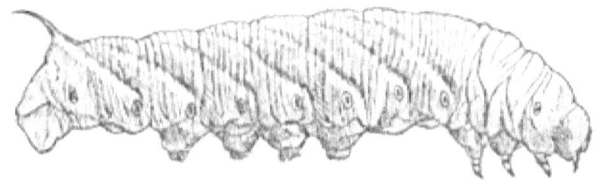

FIG. 35. LARVA OF TOMATO-WORM MOTH.

long, cylindrical case, with a long tongue-case bent backward from one end until its top touches the case, forming a handle like that of a pitcher. These chrysalids are often turned up by the plow or spade.

Remedies.—As the worms are so large and conspicuous, hand-picking is a comparatively easy and a certainly effective remedy. Kerosene emulsion (see page 9) may be effectively used in spraying.

The worms are infested by the larvæ or maggots of a small hymenopterous parasite that deposits its eggs on the worm. The maggots, on hatching, burrow into the body, living on the juices of the host, and finally coming out on the back of the worm, where they spin small, white, silken cocoons. These cocoons are conspicuous on the infested Tomato Worm.

Kansas Notes.—This pest rarely does serious damage, but is continually present over the State.

CUCUMBER BEETLE.
(*Diabrotica vittata* Fabr.; Order, Coleoptera.)

Diagnosis.—Infesting cucumbers, squashes, melons, etc.; a small, yellow, black-striped beetle, one-fourth inch long, feeding on the leaves and stems.

Description and Life-history.—The head and antennæ of the beetles are black, general body-color yellow, and a black median stripe on each wing-cover. The eggs are laid in the soil about the stem of the food-plant, and the hatched larvæ feed on the roots. These larvæ are slender, white grubs, and, when abundant, may do considerable injury. The major portion of the damage by these insects is done by the adult beetles in their feeding on the leaves. The insects pass the winter in the adult or beetle stage, under leaves, logs, and various rubbish.

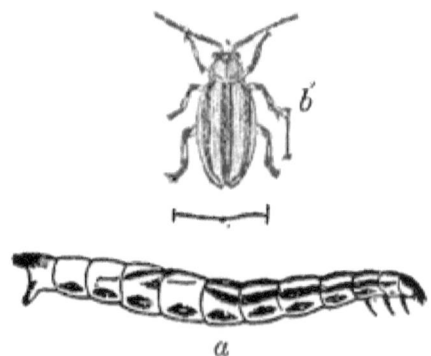

FIG. 36. CUCUMBER BEETLE; *a*, larva; *b*, adult.

Remedies.—Inclosing the young cucumber or melon vines with netting keeps the beetles from the leaves, and yet admits light and air. Wires thrust in the ground so as to form two crossing arches, like the "basket" on a croquet ground, and covered with cheese cloth or netting, do well.

Pyrethrum (see p. 9) may be applied as a powder with some dust or powder gun with excellent results. The powder should be dusted on in the morning when the dew is still on the leaves.

Kansas Notes.—This pest is at times very destructive over limited areas. This year it has been very abundant in certain Douglas county market gardens.

OTHER INSECTS ATTACKING GARDEN CROPS.

SOUTHERN CORN-ROOT WORM.
ROCKY MOUNTAIN LOCUST.
GARDEN WEB-WORM.
CORN WORM—THE TOMATO.
FALL ARMY-WORM.
INJURIOUS GRASSHOPPERS.

INSECTS ATTACKING LARGE FRUITS.

ROUND-HEADED APPLE-TREE BORER.
(*Saperda candida* Fabr.; Order, Coleoptera.)

Diagnosis.—Attacking the apple; careful examination in fall revealing a discoloration of the bark near the base of the trunk in young trees, the larvæ (first year) lying beneath the discolored bark; in spring, cracks in the bark through which castings and reddish wood dust drop. Remove the earth from the base of the trunk, gently scrape the bark, and examine carefully every unnatural-appearing spot.

Description and Life-history.—The adult insect is a beautiful beetle, belonging to the family of "long-horns" or wood-borers. It is about three-fourths of an inch long, pale brown above, with

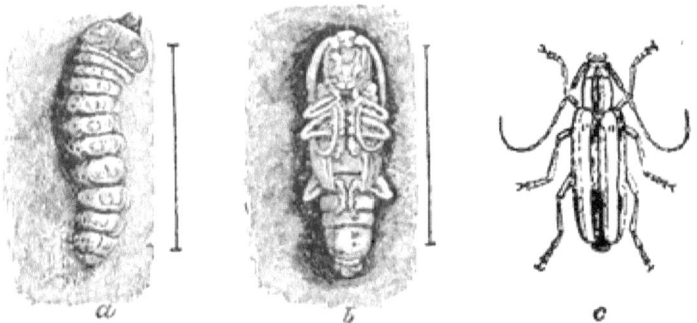

FIG. 37. ROUND-HEADED APPLE-TREE BORER; *a*, larva; *b*, pupa; *c*, adult.

two creamy-white stripes running the whole length of the body. The antennæ or feelers are almost as long as the body. The eggs are laid, according to G. C. Brackett, beneath the surface of the bark, generally at the crown (base of the trunk) or in the axis of the larger limbs, but also along the body of the trunk and large limbs. It is generally stated that the eggs are deposited on the bark (see Remedies, this insect). The eggs are deposited in Kansas from June until as late as September (Brackett), the female making a slight incision in the bark and thrusting the egg beneath one of the flaps at right angles to the cut. Most of the eggs are probably laid in June and July.

The young larvæ or borers are hatched in about two weeks, and bore into the inner bark and sap-wood, where they remain in shallow cavities for the first year of their existence, feeding until the winter months, when they move down to the lower part of

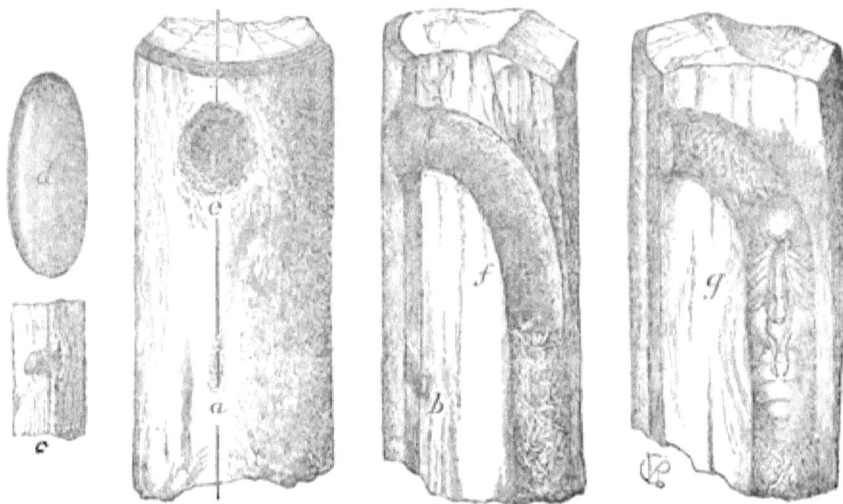

Fig. 38. Egg-laying and final exit of Round-headed Apple-tree Borer; *a*, incision where egg is laid; *b*, same, with the wood split lengthwise along the line *a*, *e*, and turned so as to show an egg in place; *c*, same, with the bark split on the same line, and removed to the left, so as to show the manner in which the egg is commonly thrust to one side under the bark; *d*, the egg, enlarged; *e*, hole of exit of beetle; *f*, the same, as it appears from the side when split along the line *a*, *e*; *g*, the burrow as it appears while the insect is in the pupa state, and before the bark is perforated.

their burrows, frequently below the surface of the ground, lying inactive till spring. In the spring the larva moves up, and feeds again on the inner bark and sap-wood until the following winter. During this second season it attains about half its growth, and does much damage to the tree by more or less completely girdling it. After another winter's rest it becomes active again, and during the third summer of its existence it cuts cylindrical channels into the heart-wood of the tree, and, in the fall, being full-grown, bores outward to the bark, lining a cavity at the end of its burrow with its castings and wood dust. In this cavity it lies inactive till the following spring, when it pupates. Finally, about the first of June, it changes to the perfect beetle and gnaws its way out through the bark.

When full-grown the larva is a little over an inch long, fleshy, footless, with a round, chestnut-brown head.

Remedies.— A preventive which has been much recommended is that of washing the base of the tree trunk with an alkaline mixture. One quart of soft soap or one pound of hard soap, with about two gallons of water and a pint of crude carbolic acid, should be mixed, and thoroughly applied with a scrub brush to the collar of the tree; some applied to the principal fork of the tree may do good. This wash is repulsive to the beetle and prevents the laying of the eggs. The wash should be applied first late in May and occasionally thereafter in June and July.

Mr. G. C. Brackett, secretary of the Kansas State Horticultural Society, claims that washes and external applications are not practically reliable as a preventive of egg-laying. (Report State Horticultural Society for 1879, p. 199.)

A tedious but sure method is that of cutting out the young larvæ. A careful examination of the tree for discolorations in the bark, and for castings issuing from the trunk, will usually reveal the whereabouts of the borers. They may be cut out with a sharp knife, or, if they have burrowed deeply, may be reached by using a stout, wire probe.

Kansas Notes.—The Round-headed Apple-tree Borer has long been recognized as, next to the Codlin Moth, perhaps, the most serious apple pest in the State. References to its presence are conspicuous in the reports of the State Horticultural Society since the beginning of their publication. This borer is a native of America, being first described by Thomas Say in 1824. It lives, also, according to Saunders, in native crab-trees, in the common June-berry, the pear, quince, and mountain ash.

FLAT-HEADED APPLE-TREE BORER.

(*Chrysobothris femorata* Fabr.; Order, Coleoptera.)

Diagnosis.—Attacking the trunk and larger branches of the apple; on examination of the trees in the fall, presence of young borers is detected by discolored spots, cracking of the bark, or sawdust-like excrement. Sickly and newly planted trees are especially liable to attack. In summer the adult beetle (three-eighths to one-half inch long, flattish, oblong, greenish-black, feet shining green) may be seen "basking in the sunshine" on the tree trunks.

Description and Life-history.—This apple pest is markedly different, in both larval and adult states, from the Round-headed Apple-tree Borer. The adult is a beetle belonging to the family Buprestidæ.

 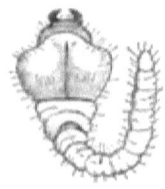

FIG. 39. FLAT-HEADED APPLE-TREE BORER; beetle and larva.

"It is of a flattish, oblong form, and of a shining, greenish-black color, each of its wing-cases [or covers] having three raised lines, the other two interrupted by two impressed transverse spots of a brassy color, dividing each wing-cover into three nearly equal portions. The under side of the body and the legs shine like burnished copper; the feet are shining green." The beetle is from three-eighths to one-half an inch long. It is seen from June 1 to the middle of August. The following notes on the life-history of the pest in Kansas are quoted from a report of the committee of entomology of the Douglas County Horticultural Society (see Kansas Horticultural Report, vol. IX (1879), p. 166; reprinted in other volumes of the reports):

Your committee beg leave to offer the following deductions from their observations of the Flat-headed Apple-tree Borer, so destructive to orchards, shade and ornamental trees, during the years 1874 and 1875, in this State:

1. This very destructive insect made its first appearance in the beetle form on May 25; were the most numerous between the middle of June and August 1. A few were seen as late as August 26.

2. They commenced depositing eggs by the middle of June, which were placed under scales and in crevices of the bark, generally upon the side exposed to the direct rays of the sun. Wounded portions, made by bruises, trimming off of branches, and sun-scalds, were found especially inviting to their deposits.

3. They infest only such trees as are debilitated. Late transplanting, protracted drouths, derangements of the organisms by extremes of heat and cold, unproductive soil, neglect in care and cultivation, produce a low condition of vitality in trees, a condition sought for by the mother of this species as most naturally adapted to a successful procreation.

4. The larva, or worm, does not survive a vigorous flow of sap, nor endure a continual shade. In the first condition it drowns, and in the second it weakens and dies.

5. It deposits its eggs during the middle of the day, and only during warm, sunny days. In the morning and evening, on stormy days and

during the night, it retires to the small branches among the dense foliage, for a cover, and is very sluggish.

6. It infests the apple, pear, cherry, plum, quince, white maple, willow, ash, tulip, and strawberry bush, and there is some evidence that the elm and cottonwood are being attacked by it.

The young larva, soon hatching from the eggs in the crevices of the bark, eats its way through the outer bark, continues for some time feeding just beneath the surface, leaving a flattened burrow filled with its sawdust-like castings. A single borer oftentimes girdles a young tree. The larva soon burrows deeper, and feeds on the inner sap-wood. While feeding beneath the bark, the presence of the larva is fairly apparent on examination, and it is at this time (in September and October) that much can be done toward ridding the trees of the pests.

The mature larva is a pale yellow, footless grub, with its anterior end greatly enlarged and flattened. When ready to pupate, the larva gnaws its way out from the sap-wood and partially through the bark. Here, in about three weeks, it changes to the adult or perfect beetle, which gnaws its way through the remaining covering of bark and escapes. The transformations of this insect are thought to take place in a year, (differing in this from the Round-headed Borer,) but this is not known with certainty.

Remedies.—As for the Round-headed Apple-tree Borer.

Several hymenopterous parasites attack this pest; woodpeckers seek out the larvæ and eat them.

The report of the Douglas County Horticultural Society committee of entomology, previously referred to, included several recommendations of remedial measures. I quote from the report as follows:

In view of the foregoing facts, your committee would recommend that all such varieties of trees found liable to the attacks of this insect should be planted in the spring as early as the ground can be placed in suitable condition to receive them; and to facilitate early planting, fall plowing and preparation is advisable; that vigorous trees, carefully dug so as to preserve a large amount of the roots, be obtained in the fall and properly trenched in upon the premises, handy for planting. As soon as set, remove a large portion of the last year's growth. Mulch the ground for the space of two feet around—three or four feet would be better—and wrap the bodies with some cheap material, as newspapers, hay, or old rags. Plant no crops among them which will prevent constant and thorough cultivation of the ground, and especially leave ample room on each side of the rows for the free use of the plow without endangering the roots or chafing the bodies and branches. This care in planting, followed with constant cultivation, will produce a strong, vigorous growth, which of itself is the most complete safeguard against the attacks of this borer.

If through ignorance or neglect trees already planted have become infested during the year previous, the only method of combating it is to destroy the beetle as soon as it comes forth from its burrow. The time, as stated, of its first appearance is the last of May; and at this time the search should begin, and be kept up unceasingly and thoroughly through the season, or until the last one has been captured and destroyed. As alleged in deduction No. 5, the beetle is active only during the middle of sunny days, and in the morning and evening and during cloudy and stormy days it is sluggish. A touch even, or a jarring of the trees will frequently cause it to drop to the ground, and, opossom-like, it will appear as dead for a moment, and is easily killed. But in the middle of the day, when the sun has warmed it, it is very active and quick to run, often taking to the wing to escape at the first approach of man. However, if approached from the opposite side of the tree, a quick slap of the hand, covering it, will destroy in most attempts. Generally it will be found upon the southern side of the tree, basking in the sun's warmth, though at the approach of man it will often quickly glide to the opposite side to conceal itself from sight. All sides should be carefully examined.

Your committee would especially call your attention to deductions Nos. 2 and 4. In No. 2 it is stated that sun-scalds are favorite spots, inviting the attack of this borer, and in No. 4, that it does not seek, nor can endure, a continual shade. These two facts furnish a strong argument in favor of low heads and a shady growth as requisites of successful orcharding in this climate, as sun-scalds seldom occur upon trees of such a form, nor will such a growth furnish congenial conditions for the existence of the progeny of the flat-heads. As it is not presumable that all the beetles will be captured, it will become necessary to examine the trees for the purpose of destroying the worms hatched from the eggs which the uncaptured beetle may deposit. To detect their whereabouts is to the inexperienced quite a difficult undertaking. Until late in summer or early in autumn, no external marks indicate their presence save a small speck, or sometimes a dark line, so fine that they will not attract the attention of those not understanding the cause as being anything injurious to the trees. It will be necessary for such persons to examine into every unnatural-looking spot the eye may detect. Experience will soon remove the necessity for so close and careful examination and enable one to detect what are the reliable markings indicating their presence. In this work a sharp knife is all that is needed, *if begun in proper time*, as they will be found in and just under the bark, until about September 1, when the first ones hatched will commence to penetrate the wood. In cases where they have entered the wood, a probe made of common broom wire is all-sufficient with which to thrust them through or drag them from their holes. If, after several thrusts, a milky substance is discovered at the extremity of the probe, it is safe to conclude that a fatal stab has been given the worm, and you can pass to the next. They will be found the most numerous along the margins of wounds and new formations, healing places, where branches have been cut off, and upon the side of those branches having an exposure to the sun. Branches which have become bent by a heavy load of fruit are liable to their attacks upon the upper side, as the sap becomes sluggish in such places.

Kansas Notes—This borer is a native American insect, and is found all over the country. It is mentioned in the Transactions of the Kansas Horticultural Society for 1873. (See pp. 123 and 133.) In the Transactions of the Society for 1874, Mr. G. C. Brackett says (p. 194):

> This of all others has been the most troublesome to the orchardist during the past season, and the most difficult to combat. . . . Row after row of fine and promising young orchards throughout the State have been literally cut to pieces by their silent and incessant gnawing.

In the report of the committee of entomology, Kansas State Horticultural Society for 1884, (see Report of Kansas State Horticultural Society for 1885, p. 102,) it is said:

> This insect is of very general distribution throughout the State, and seems to be present wherever apple trees are planted. It breeds in many of our native fruit-trees, and it will probably be always with us. . . . In some localities the loss occasioned by it is very great. H. E. VanDeman estimates its injuries as equal to 25 per cent. of the trees in our orchards. L. A. Simmons writes that "it has destroyed many thousands of trees, the year they were planted." G. W. Ashby calls it "the terror of the orchardist." Many others mention it as being destructive to young or neglected orchards.

APPLE-ROOT LOUSE.

(*Schizoneura lanigera* Hausm.; Order, Hemiptera.)

Diagnosis.—Infesting apple; starving and weakening, sometimes dying trees, with no indication of borers, nor any visible insect pests at work; on examination of the roots, small, wart-like swellings of all shapes and sizes, and in these swellings minute plant-lice covered with bluish-white "wool."

Description and Life-history.—This insect is one of the plant-lice, minute, soft-bodied, mostly wingless insects which live by sucking plant juices. They have fine, sharp-pointed, sucking beaks. Under the microscope, the beak of the Apple-root Louse will be found to be about three-fourths as long as the body of the louse, and it is usually folded back under the body. With this beak the lice puncture the root and rootlets of the tree, sucking

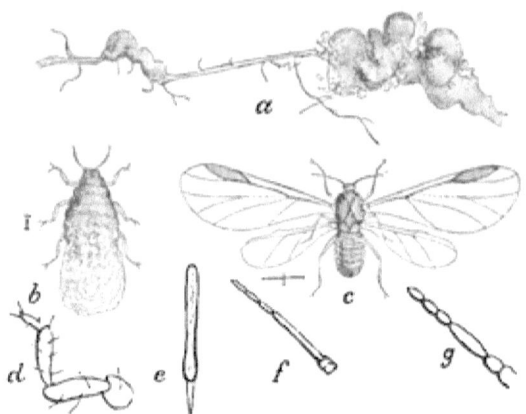

FIG. 40. APPLE-ROOT LOUSE: *a*, infested root; *b*, young; *c*, winged adult; *d*, a leg; *e*, the sucking beak; *f*, antenna of adult; *g*, antenna of young.

from them the nourishing juices and seriously impoverishing the tree. The swellings are expansions of the root tissue, caused by the irritation of the punctures.

The lice sometimes ascend from the roots and attack the branches, gathering in groups on the tender bark. They may easily be recognized here by the white cottony or woolly covering of their bodies.

Remedies.—The Apple-root Louse has many natural enemies, as have all plant-lice. Several predaceous beetles, conspicuous among them certain "lady-birds" (little sub-hemispherical beetles), and the footless maggots of various two-winged flies (Syrphidæ), consider the soft-bodied lice to be dainty tid-bits.

Scalding water (temperature not exceeding 150° F.) poured freely over the infested roots is the best remedy yet devised. The roots may be laid bare and the hot water freely poured over them without injury. A mulch placed around the trees will bring many of the lice to the surface, when the hot water may be effectively applied. Drenching the roots with soap-suds followed by a liberal dressing of wood ashes is recommended.

Dr. Lintner, State Entomologist of New York, finds that two

or three pounds of gas lime distributed over the surface of the soil within a radius of four feet from the tree, trusting to rain to carry the lime into the soil, is very effective. Mr. N. P. Deming, of Douglas county, adopts this method (I believe he was not aware of Dr. Lintner's recommendation, but devised it for himself) with good results.

Young trees from the nursery, which are found to be infested, should have their roots dipped into weak lye. Concerning infested nursery stock, I quote the following sensible and vigorous remarks from Mr. G. C. Brackett (Report State Horticultural Society for 1879, p. 173):

> To nurserymen let the injunction be given, and doubly emphasized, that, for their own reputations' sake as honorable, intelligent and "square" men, having the highest regard for the horticultural interests of our State, and an honest desire for the success of those engaged in rearing orchards, they should never allow trees infested with this louse to go from their grounds — not even for thrice the price of clean trees — thereby scattering the seed that shall cause an incalculable injury, and losses of the most serious character; and the nurseryman who is not well informed with reference to the insects and their habits, which infest the trees and plants which he propagates and offers for sale in the market, is disqualified for the pursuit, has mistaken his calling, and there exists no apology for him.

Kansas Notes.—This apple pest has been, as the Apple-tree Borers, known in Kansas almost since apple growing began. In 1848 it was abundant in the eastern United States, and since then has become disseminated over the whole country. In the Report of the Kansas State Horticultural Society for 1880 (p. 176), it is reported as having seriously injured the trees of a fruit-grower in Franklin county "for several years past."

SPRING CANKER-WORM.
(*Anisopteryx vernata* Peck; Order, Lepidoptera.)

Diagnosis.—Attacking the apple; many grayish measuring-worms, about an inch long, defoliating the trees in the spring; when disturbed, the worms let themselves down from the branches, suspended by silken threads; when walking, move with a looping or measuring motion.

Description and Life-history.—The adult insect is a brownish-gray moth (male), with wings expanding about one inch. The fore wings have darker markings, and the hind wings are light gray with a dusky central dot. The female is wingless, having a peculiar, spider-like appearance. She is from three- to four-tenths of an inch in length.

The moths issue in early spring from chrysalids which have passed the winter in the ground. The female crawls up the tree and deposits her eggs in small masses on the twigs or branches. The young larvæ or caterpillars issue just as the leaves begin to unfold from the bud. The young larva is "dark olive-green or brown in color, with a black, shining head." The larvæ feed voraciously, and in Kansas are usually full-grown by the middle of May, when they enter the ground to pupate. They remain in the ground as chrysalids until the following spring; a few, however, probably issue in the fall of the first year. The larva or "worm" is about one inch long; the head mottled and spotted; the body is longitudinally striped with many pale lines. When in large numbers, this pest may so completely defoliate an orchard as to leave the trees as if swept by fire. Two or three successive visitations of the pest in large numbers generally kill the infested trees.

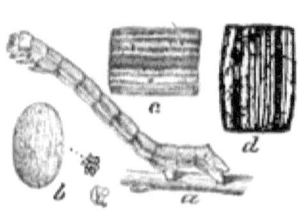

FIG. 41. SPRING CANKER-WORM; *a*, larva; *b*, magnified egg and a small cluster of eggs; *c*, magnified portion of side of larva, and *d*, same of back, showing markings.

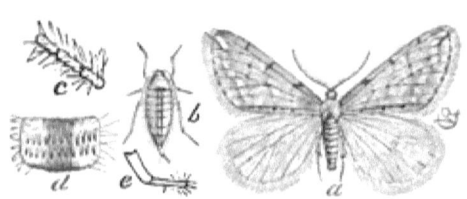

FIG. 42. SPRING CANKER-WORM; *a*, male moth; *b*, female moth; *c*, joints of antenna of female moth; *d*, joint of abdomen of female moth; *e*, retractile ovipositor of female.

Remedies.—The Canker-worm is a great favorite with insectivorous birds, more than fifty species of birds which feed on the worms being enumerated by Maynard.

Spraying with London purple (see p. 8) or Paris green (see p. 7) is probably the most effective remedy. The spraying should be done soon after the worms hatch.

Preventing the ascent of the wingless female up the tree trunks to lay her eggs may be accomplished by encircling the tree with a narrow band of some sticky substance, as refuse sorghum molasses, printer's ink, pine tar, etc. The sticky substance should be spread on a canvas or paper band tied tightly around the tree trunk. The application should be made in the first mild days of spring, and the band kept sticky by frequent renewals until the leaves are started on the tree.

If the Canker-worms are once thoroughly exterminated in an orchard, they may not reappear for a long time. Owing to the wingless condition of the females, the pest spreads slowly; but for this very reason a local attack largely increases in strength with each succeeding year, the females of each succeeding generation being confined to a limited range.

Kansas Notes.—Mr. G. C. Brackett, in the Transactions Kansas State Horticultural Society for 1873, says (p. 114):

. . . There is not any reason, judging from the past, to believe that they [Canker-worms] will ever become so numerous in this climate as to do us any material injury. I have not seen it here only in a very few instances, and am of the opinion that in these few cases the eggs had been introduced upon trees brought from the more northern and eastern States. They continued one season, and, from some debilitating cause, weakened and died out.

The first serious occurrence in Kansas of this pest was in 1879, in the large orchard of D. W. Houston, in Anderson county. (See Report State Horticultural Society for 1880, p. 169; also, Report State Horticultural Society for 1882, p. 154.) This orchard consisted of 4,000 trees. In 1879, first appearance, they defoliated 300 trees; the following year they defoliated 3,000 trees in the same orchard, "leaving the trees," to use Colonel Houston's words, "as bare of foliage as they were in January."

They next appeared in Neosho, Allen, Woodson, Montgomery, Chautauqua and Douglas counties. The following year they were observed in Osage, Coffey, Wilson and Elk counties in addition, and in that portion of the State embraced by the lower Neosho and Verdigris rivers and their tributaries the injuries were very severe. In 1884, the worms did not appear in such abundance in the infested region.

CODLIN MOTH.

(*Carpocapsa pomonella* Linn.; Order, Lepidoptera.)

Diagnosis.—Infesting the apple (in fruit); while the apples are on the tree, small masses of reddish-brown castings protruding from a hole on the side of the apple or at the eye (the end opposite the stalk end); on cutting into these apples, a soft, flesh-colored, brown-headed, sixteen-legged larva or grub, boring and eating around the core. Many infested apples fall to the ground; from these apples the grubs have usually escaped. In the winter many small, tough cocoons on the apple barrels (between hoops and staves).

Description and Life-history.—The Codlin Moth is probably the most seriously injurious of apple pests. The adult is a small, ashy-gray and brown moth, its wings expanding about three-fourths of an inch. Each fore wing has a large, oval, tawny-brown spot on its hinder margin. The moths appear about May 1, from hibernating chrysalids, and lay their eggs singly at the blossom ends of the young apples. The egg hatches in about one week, and the young larva begins eating its way into the core. The newly-hatched grub is white, with blackish head. As it grows older and larger the body becomes pinkish or flesh-colored, and the head brown. When full-grown, it measures about three-fourths of an inch in length The castings are pushed out of the entrance hole at the blossom end of the apple, or a new and larger hole is made at the side of the fruit. The ·larvæ become full-grown in three or four weeks after hatching, by which time the infested fruit has gener-

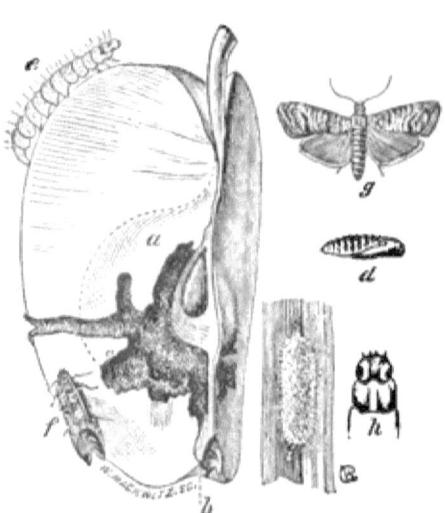

FIG. 43. CODLIN MOTH: *a*, section of infested apple, showing burrows and channel of exit; *b*, point of egg-laying, and entrance of young larva; *c*, larva; *h*, head and first segment of larva, enlarged; *i*, the cocoon; *d*, chrysalis, which is inclosed in the cocoon; *f, g,* moth.

ally fallen to the ground. The first grubs begin to leave the apples in Kansas about the first of June. They spin up and pupate in crevices in the bark of the apple trees, and the adult moths issue in about two weeks. These moths lay eggs on the later apples, and another brood of grubs does what damage it can. These larvæ mature in the fall, but do not pupate, invariably passing the winter in the larval state either within the stored apples, or within a cocoon on the tree, or in the store-house. They pupate in early spring, and issue as moths about the first of May. The insect is thus two-brooded. Besides the apple, it is known to attack the pear, plum, and peach. There is usually but a single grub to an apple; as many as four or five have been found in one fruit, however.

Remedies.—As most of the infested apples fall to the ground before the grub escapes, gathering and destroying the apples, as soon as fallen (the larva soon escapes from the fallen fruit), is an effective remedy.

Trapping the insects, by providing places for them in which to spin up, is very effectual. Bands of wrapping paper or rags should be tied about the tree trunks about the first of June. They should be visited weekly, or once in 10 days, and the spun-up larvæ or chrysalids destroyed. The paper bands can be taken off and burned; if rags are used, they may be scalded and then replaced. That the larvæ may be induced to frequent these bands, the rough bark should be scraped from the trunk, and all rubbish and weeds should be cleared from the ground near the trees.

As many of the second brood of larvæ are stored with the winter apples, the barrels should be carefully examined during the winter and all hibernating larvæ (within cocoons) found should be killed.

Spraying with London purple (see p. 8) against this pest has been tested and pronounced a valuable remedial measure. The spraying should be done at the time of the first falling of the blossoms, when the calyces are turned up, forming so many little cups on the blossom ends of the fruits, into which the poison falls. The newly-hatched larvæ endeavoring to penetrate the forming fruit are killed. The spraying should be repeated in 10 days or two weeks after the first application. One pound of London purple should be mixed with 250 gallons of water.

Kansas Notes.—This pest is of foreign origin, having been imported into this country from Europe about the beginning of this century. It has spread all over North America, and is, perhaps, our most destructive apple pest. Professor Popenoe has estimated the damage in Kansas orchards sometimes to amount to two-thirds of the crop. The pest has been known in Kansas since apples began to bear. It was first noticeable near Missouri river towns, and gradually spread over the State, following railroads and other lines of travel. It is transported chiefly by the shipment of wormy fruit.

It is mentioned constantly in the published transactions and reports of the State Horticultural Society since the first meeting of the society, in 1871.

TARNISHED PLANT-BUG.

(*Lygus lineolaris* P. Beauv.; Order, Hemiptera.)

Diagnosis.—Attacking the apple, pear, quince, plum, cherry, strawberry, and many herbaceous plants; a small, dark-brown to yellowish-brown sucking bug, one-fifth of an inch long, (head yellowish, with three narrow, reddish stripes; thorax yellow-margined, with several yellow, longitudinal lines, a more or less distinct yellow V-mark behind the thorax;) attacking the buds, young leaves, and young fruit.

Description and Life-history.—The insect hibernates in the adult state, finding shelter beneath leaves, in rubbish, etc., and coming out during the first warm days of early spring. The flying bugs appear with the first vegetation. They bury themselves among the expanding buds, or in the blossoms, and suck the life juices of the plant. Affected fruit buds appear as if frost-bitten. The blossoms of apple trees are a favorite feeding ground of this pest. The eggs are laid on the food-plant, and the young bugs appear as early as the middle of April and first of May. The young resemble the adult in shape, (see description in Diagnosis, this insect,) but are green, and lack

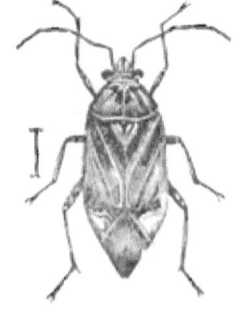

FIG. 44. TARNISHED PLANT-BUG.

wings or have very short ones. There are two, and perhaps more, broods in a season (Weed). In the fall, only mature individuals are found; at this time they frequent golden-rods, sunflowers, asters, and other fall flowers. The injuries to fruit-trees are done in the spring; "buttoning" of strawberries is often caused by this pest (Weed).

Remedies.—Kerosene emulsion or pyrethrum (see p. 9) prove effective. Arsenical poisons cannot be used, of course, as the insect does not eat the leaves, but sucks the juices from them.

By shaking the infested trees in spring, early in the morning, when the bugs are sluggish, many may be captured and destroyed.

Kansas Notes.—In the Transactions of the Kansas State Horticultural Society for 1873, Prof. E. A. Popenoe reports seeing many Tarnished Plant-bugs in the blossoms of apple trees. They have been observed continuously since, and certainly do considerable harm annually.

APPLE-TREE TWIG BORER.
(*Amphicerus bicaudatus* Say; Order. Coleoptera.)

Diagnosis.—Infesting the apple; leaves turning brown, and small twigs withering; on examination, small holes found near buds, usually in the axils, from six inches to a foot from the end of the twig; the twigs break off freely in high winds.

Description and Life-history.—This pest is a small, cylindrical, dark-brown beetle, from one-fourth to one-third of an inch long. The injury is mostly done by the adult, which bores into small branches of apple, pear, cherry, sumac, and grape, and digs a cylindrical burrow within the branch one or two inches long. The life-history of this pest has been studied by Prof. E. A. Popenoe. For a considerable time after the insect had been recognized as a pest of fruit-trees, the life-history and the character of the early stages were unknown. Professor Popenoe concludes from his studies that the beetle is single-brooded, hibernating in the adult state, emerging in the spring (April and May), and depositing eggs in unhealthy or dead wood of grape-vines and tamarix. The larvæ on hatching bore into the canes and make cylindrical burrows.

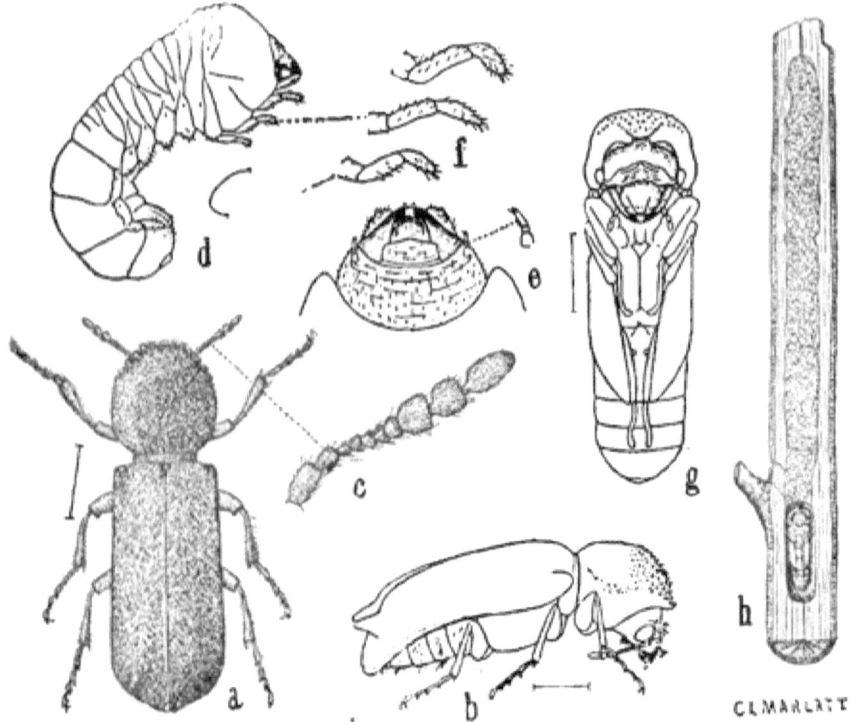

FIG. 45. TRANSFORMATIONS OF THE APPLE-TWIG BORER; the figures, excepting *b*, which is natural size, are enlarged, the hair-lines at the side, in *a*, *b*, *d*, and *g*, showing the actual size; *a*, the female beetle from above; *b*, outline side view of male beetle; *c*, antenna, showing structure; *d*, full-grown larva; *e*, head and antenna, and *f*, the right legs of the larva; *g*, front view of pupa, in outline; *h*, twig, showing, above, the larval burrow packed with castings, and below, the pupa in its cell.

The larvæ transform to pupæ in the burrows, and the insect matures in the fall or winter. The beetles burrow into fruit and forest trees for protection and food, and may be found in them head downward.

The injuries done by the pest are to grape canes, into which it bores as larvæ, and to orchard trees, into which it bores as adult beetles.

Remedies.—The dying twigs in winter, caused by the beetles' burrows, should be collected and burned, thus destroying many adults.

All prunings, diseased and dead vines, should be carefully collected in the vineyard and destroyed, thus taking away sought-for breeding-places, and also, if done in the summer, destroying many larvæ.

Kansas Notes.—In Report Kansas State Horticultural Society for 1885, Mr. A. N. Godfrey mentions it (p. 163) as an apple pest, but says "it is never seriously injurious."

In the First Annual Report of the Kansas Experiment Station, State Agricultural College, for 1888, Prof. E. A. Popenoe (p. 209 et seq.) writes of this pest. Referring to its presence in Kansas, he says:

Among the numerous insects concerning which information has been asked during the season past, none, seemingly, has attracted more general attention than the Apple-twig Borer. Specimens of the insect, and its work in grape-vines and apple twigs, have reached us from various points in eastern and central Kansas, Norton and Lane being the westernmost counties from which complaints are noted.

In a letter, with specimens, to this department last May, a correspondent at Solomon Rapids, Mitchell county, says: "I fear they will destroy my orchard." However, not much fear for old trees need be entertained. Most of the injury is done in the nursery and in recently-set-out orchards.

FALL WEB-WORM.
(*Hyphantria textor* Harris; Order, Lepidoptera.)

Diagnosis.—Attacking the apple; caterpillars about an inch long or less, pale yellowish to bluish-black, covered with tufts of long, yellowish hairs, arising from small, black or orange-yellow protuberances; feeding in swarms within large webs, occasionally outside of the webs, in late summer and early autumn (not in spring); attacking, also, other fruit-trees and forest trees.

Description and Life-history.—The adult insect is a milk-white, unspotted moth, measuring about 1¼ inches from tip to tip of expanded wings. It flies at night. The eggs are laid in patches on the under sides of the leaves, in June. The larvæ issue in July and August, and immediately spin a web inclosing the group. They eat only the soft portion of the leaves, leaving the veins and under skin untouched. The young larva is pale yellowish, with scattering hairs, black head, and a longitudinal stripe on each side of the body, yellow interrupted by black speckles. They feed voraciously, and when full-grown suddenly leave the webs and scatter over the tree. The full-grown larva has a greenish-yellow ground color, with velvety-black back. The sides are speckled with black, except for two yellow stripes. Beneath, dusty or smoky-brown. Covered with dusty-white to reddish-brown, long, straight hairs, in tufts rising from "warts." The general color varies somewhat — in some, black predominating, in others yellow.

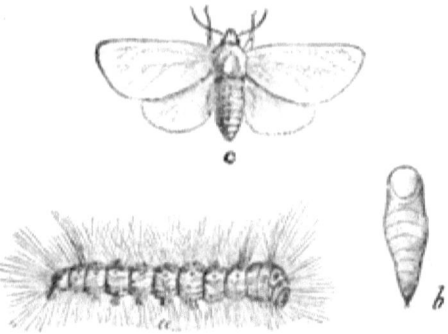

FIG. 46. FALL WEB-WORM; *a*, larva; *b*, pupa; *c*, adult.

When ready to pupate (in September and October [Saunders]), the larvæ descend to the ground, and, burrowing into it a few inches, change to chrysalids within delicate silken cocoons. They pass the winter in the pupal stage, the moths emerging in May and June.

The Fall Web-worm is easily distinguishable from the Tent Caterpillar, which it resembles in its web-making habits, by the following contrasted points in the life-history of the two species:

"The Fall Web-worm hibernates in the pupal state; appears mostly in the fall; its eggs are deposited on the leaf, and hatch before the leaf falls; it feeds on the parenchyma (filling) of the leaf under its web. The Tent Caterpillar hibernates in the egg state, and the worm hatches in the spring; the moth is reddish-brown; its eggs are deposited around a twig, because they have to pass the winter, and would get lost with the leaves if deposited upon them; it devours the whole leaf outside of its tent."

Remedies.—The immediate betrayal of the presence of the worms, by the conspicuous, unsightly webs, renders their destruction merely a matter of persistent work. The web-infested limbs may be cut off and the worms burned or crushed; or, if taking off the limbs is objectionable, the worms may be crushed within the webs with gloved hands.

Kansas Notes.—In Transactions Kansas State Horticultural Society for 1873, Mr. Brackett reports (p. 119): "Fall Web-worms are becoming quite frequent and numerous. They feed on leaves of apple, maple, willow, quince, and I have seen them on the wild plum, the oak, and the Osage orange." In the Report of Kansas

State Horticultural Society for 1882, Mr. A. N. Godfrey says of this pest:

> During the late summer months our forest trees became partially covered with a thick web, spun among the outer branches and terminal shoots. . . . The Web-worm is found on most of our forest and fruit-trees, but seems to prefer the hickory and walnut among the former, and the pear among the latter.

APPLE-TREE TENT CATERPILLAR.

(*Clisiocampa americana* Harris; Order, Lepidoptera.)

Diagnosis.—Hairy, blackish caterpillars, two inches or less in length; white stripe along the back; feeding on the leaves in May and June; silken webs or "tents" in which the caterpillars lie at night, on stormy days, and at other times when not feeding.

Description and Life-history.—The adult is a reddish-brown moth, with conspicuously (male) or inconspicuously (female) feathered antennæ; expanse of wings about 1½ inches. The moth appears in June, and is unprovided with developed mouth-parts. It deposits its eggs and soon dies. The eggs are deposited in masses of two or three hundred, arranged in "ring-like clusters" on the twigs. The egg mass is covered with a sort of varnish unaffected by rain. The larvæ do not come from the eggs until the following spring, hatching about May 1, at the time the first leaf buds are expanding. They feed five or six weeks before becoming full-grown. The "tents" are spun immediately after hatching, and enlarged, or new ones spun as necessary. The full-grown larvæ are

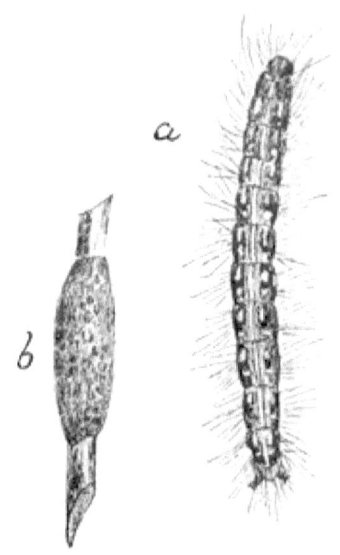

FIG. 47. APPLE-TREE TENT CATERPILLAR; *a*, larva; *b*, cluster of eggs around twig.

almost two inches long, "hairy and black, with a white stripe down the back, and on each side of this central stripe there are a number of short, irregular, longitudinal, yellow lines. On the sides are paler lines, with spots and streaks of pale blue. The under side of the body is nearly black." The "tents" are irregular in form, and have openings in the angles which serve as entrance and exit ways for the caterpillars. "It is estimated that each larva, when approaching maturity, will consume two leaves in a day; so that every day that a nest of such marauders is permitted to remain on a tree there is a sacrifice of about 500 leaves" (Saunders). When full-grown and ready to pupate, the larvæ spin yellowish, double-webbed cocoons in protected spots (such as "the angles formed by the projection of the cap boards of fences or fence posts"), and change to brown chrysalids. The following May the moths emerge.

Remedies.—As the caterpillars are all in the tents at night and rarely go out to feed before 9 A. M. (Saunders), they may be easily destroyed. Cut off the web-infested branches with the inclosed caterpillars, and burn or crush the tent and contents, or crush with gloved hands without cutting off the branch. Several parasitic ichneumon flies do much toward keeping the pest in check.

Kansas Notes.—In the Transactions Kansas State Horticultural Society for 1873, the Tent Caterpillar is mentioned as a common orchard pest. In the report of the committee on entomology, Transactions State Horticultural Society for 1874, Mr. G. C. Brackett says (p. 192): "This worm, Apple-tree Tent Caterpillar, so familiar to every orchardist, has been less numerous, either among trees in the orchards and fruit-trees, or among forest trees, than during many seasons previous." In the same Transactions, Mr. G. Y. Johnson, speaking for the eastern half of Douglas county, says (p. 208): "The Tent Caterpillar has entirely disappeared from this locality," which may be traced most directly to the agency of the ichneumon fly.

Since 1874, rare mention is made of this pest in horticultural reports, and the parasites have undoubtedly succeeded in keeping it in check.

PLUM CURCULIO.

(*Conotrachelus nenuphar* Herbst.; Order, Coleoptera.)

Diagnosis.—Diseased and gummy, unripe plums falling to the ground; within these plums a small, white, soft, footless grub. Many of the plums hanging in the tree marked with a small, crescent-shaped slit.

Description and Life-history.—This is the most formidable plum pest of this country. The adult insect is a "small, rough, grayish-black beetle about one-fifth of an inch long, with a black, shining hump on the middle of each wing-case, and behind this a more or less distinct band of a dull, ochre-yellow color, with some whitish marks about the middle." The beetle belongs to the family of curculios or snouted beetles; the snout of our plum weevil is rather short, but yet easily made out.

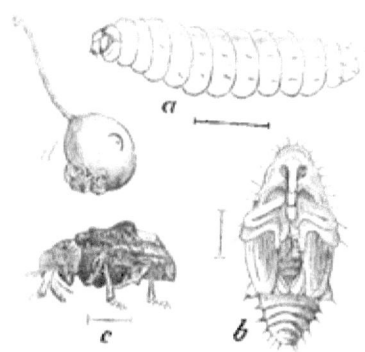

FIG. 48. PLUM CURCULIO: *a*, larva; *b*, pupa; *c*, adult; *d*, plum, showing puncture and crescent made in egg laying.

The eggs are laid in the young, green fruit shortly after it is formed. The female cuts through the skin of the fruit with her jaws, which are at the tip of the snout. She then enlarges this hole, deposits an egg in it, pushing the egg well into the hole with her snout. She next cuts a small, crescent-shaped slit in front of the hole, so as to undermine the egg and leave it in a sort of flap. The object of the crescent slit is probably to wilt the flap, and thus prevent the growing fruit from crushing the egg. The female lays from 50 to 100 eggs. The larva, as soon as hatched, begins to feed upon the pulp of the fruit, boring a winding channel to the center, where it feeds around the stone. The larva, full-grown, is about two-fifths of an inch long, soft, glassy white, with light-brown head and without feet. The infested fruit usually drops off and falls to the ground before the larva finishes its feeding. Within the fallen plum the larva completes its growth, crawls out and into the ground for several inches, and changes to pupa. After three or four weeks it emerges as an adult weevil (beetle).

The insect is single-brooded. The egg-laying begins about the middle of May and is continued by succeeding individuals for about two months. The insects mostly pass the winter in the beetle stage, a few, however, entering the ground so late that they hibernate as larvæ. The damage to the fruit is caused almost wholly by the larvæ, although both male and female beetles feed upon the fruit.

Besides the plum, this curculio attacks the peach, nectarine, apricot, apple, pear, and cherry, but not to the alarming extent as in the case of the plum.

Remedies.—The most effectual and practical remedy is one based on the observation of a peculiar habit of the plum weevil, namely, that of its folding up its legs, feigning death, and dropping when slightly jarred. What is necessary, then, is to jar the infested trees, having provided means for catching the beetles as they fall from the branches and fruit. A sheet may be spread under the tree, and the trees jarred by hand, if small; if large, by cutting off a branch, leaving a stump several inches long, and striking the end of this stump with a mallet.

Doctor Hull's "curculio catcher" is an excellent contrivance for using the jarring method. "It consists of a wheelbarrow on which is mounted a large, inverted umbrella, split in front to receive the trunk of a tree, against which the machine, which is provided with a padded bumper, is driven with force sufficient to jar the curculios down into the umbrella, where they are collected and destroyed."

Spraying with Paris green (three ounces to 50 gallons of water, see p. 7) three or four times, at intervals of a week, beginning as soon as the blossoms have fallen, may be successfully used.

Hens with their broods will do good work in an infested plum orchard. Hogs turned into the orchard will devour much of the infested fallen fruit.

Kansas Notes.—The Plum Curculio has practically prevented all plum growing in Kansas. Mr. G. C. Brackett refers to its presence in Kansas in 1873 (see Transactions State Horticultural Society 1873, p. 117).

PLUM GOUGER.

(*Coccotorus scutellaris* Lec.; Order. Coleoptera.)

Diagnosis.—Much as for Plum Curculio; differing in this, that there is no crescent-shaped split in the hanging or fallen plum, and that the grub within the fallen plum will be found within the kernel (rarely so with *Conotrachelus*). Plums attacked by the gouger become gummy and diseased, but do not so readily drop to the ground as when attacked by *Conotrachelus*.

Description and Life-history.—The adult gouger is a "snout-beetle" about one-fourth of an inch long, yellowish in color (especially on thorax and legs), and without humps on the back, as with *Conotrachelus*. It appears about the same time as *Conotrachelus*, and deposits its eggs in the young fruit. A small, round hole is made, instead of a crescent-shaped slit. The young larva soon hatches, and burrows straight for the kernel, through the soft shell of which it penetrates, and feeds upon the contents until full-grown. "The larva is of a milk-white color, with a large, horny, yellowish-white head, and jaws tipped with brown."

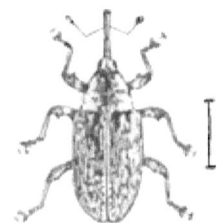

FIG. 49. PLUM GOUGER.

The pupal stage is passed within the plum stone, from which the mature beetle escapes in August or September. "While the normal habit of the Plum Curculio is to feed on the flesh outside the plum stone, which latter it only occasionally penetrates, the Plum Gouger lives and matures within." The insect hibernates in the adult or beetle stage.

Remedies.—Jarring in the manner prescribed for the Plum Curculio is pretty effective; these beetles do not drop so readily, however, as the curculios. The gougers also take wing more readily, and thus may escape. In fact, this pest is decidedly more difficult to deal with than the other, but it is rarely as numerous, and is by no means so widely spread.

Kansas Notes.—"The Plum Gouger seems to be unknown in the Eastern States, or, at least, is not common there; but it is very generally distributed throughout the valley of the Mississippi" (Riley).

CHERRY APHIS.

(*Myzus cerasi* Fabr.; Order, Hemiptera.)

Diagnosis.—Twigs and under surface of leaves of the cherry spotted or covered with great numbers in groups of minute, shining, black insects. Leaves wilt; growth of tree is stunted.

Description and Life-history.—This pest is one of the plant-lice or aphids, minute, soft-bodied, most of the individuals wingless, sucking insects. (For general appearance, see Figs. 10 and 11.) It passes the winter in the egg state, on the cherry twigs; early in spring the young aphids, hatching, gather on the bursting buds and begin sucking the juice from the unfolding leaves. In a week or 10 days the plant-lice are mature, and begin giving birth to young, which, in turn, are soon fully developed. The plant-lice increase in numbers with marvelous rapidity, and if not checked by the attacks of many natural enemies would soon overrun all vegetation. The young are born alive, except in the case of the first brood of the year, which issue from eggs laid by the last brood of the preceding year. This last fall brood is composed of winged individuals, most of the other broods being wingless.

Remedies.—The natural enemies of the plant-lice, including lady-birds and their larvæ, parasitic two- and four-winged flies, etc., are usually sufficient to keep the aphids in check.

Kerosene emulsion (see p. 9) sprayed on the lice is the most effective artificial remedy. As the lice live by sucking, poisoning the foliage is unavailing. The insecticide must be something which will destroy the insects by actual contact. Strong soap-suds or tobacco water are recommended.

Kansas Notes.—The Cherry Aphis is perhaps not a formidable insect enemy to orchardists of this State, yet it undoubtedly does some annual damage in stunting the spring growth of young trees.

I have seen young cherry trees with large portions of their fresh leaves and tender shoots fairly covered and blackened by these insects.

PEACH-TREE BORER.

(*Egeria exitiosa* Say: Order, Lepidoptera.)

Diagnosis.—Attacking the peach; the tree, badly attacked, giving indications of approaching death; at the base of the trunk, next to the ground and just below it, and on the large roots (examined by uncovering them), gummy exudations mingled with wood dust. On cutting into the root, following one of these gummy burrows, a naked, soft, pale whitish-yellow, sixteen-footed grub about one-half inch long is found.

Description and Life-history.—The adult insect is a beautiful, clear-winged, day-flying moth, with glossy, steel-blue body, crossed by a broad band of orange-yellow. The wings expand about 1½ inches.

The eggs are laid on the bark of the tree, at the surface of the ground, during the summer. The larvæ, soon hatching, burrow in and down to the inner bark and sap-wood of the larger roots, upon which they feed. Their burrowing causes a profuse exudation of gum, which, mixed with the wood dust, produces a noticeable mass around the roots of the tree.

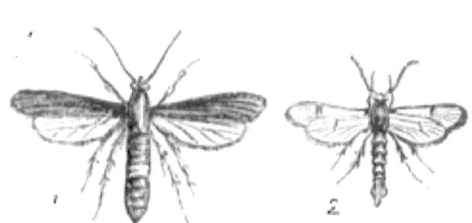

FIG. 50. PEACH-TREE BORER: 1, female; 2, male.

The larva, when full-grown, is fully half an inch long, soft, cylindrical, pale whitish-yellow, with horny, reddish head and strong, black jaws. It has eight pairs of feet, and there are a few scattered hairs on the otherwise naked body.

The larvæ continue feeding for nearly a year, interrupted only by the winter months. When ready to pupate, the larva crawls upward nearly to the surface of the ground and builds a tight case of silk, gum, and its own castings, within which it pupates. The pupal state lasts about three weeks. The moth then issues, and the eggs are laid. The larva enters the pupal state in southern Kansas in April (see D. Doyle, Report Kansas State Horticultural Society, 1885, p. 12), and appears as an adult (the moth) in May and June.

The larvæ may be found of many different sizes at any one time. Although there is but one generation a year, the larvæ mature at such different times that "they keep up a nearly constant supply of imagines."

Remedies.—The most effective remedy is the cutting out of the larvæ. Early in the spring the base of the trunk and the large roots should be uncovered and examined. The presence of the gummy exudations indicates the whereabouts of the burrows. The larvæ should be dug out with a sharp knife.

As a preventive remedy "mounding" is highly recommended. In spring before the moths emerge (April), dirt is thrown up around the tree about a foot high and pressed firmly about the trunk. The moths are thus prevented from laying their eggs at the base of the trunk. Some fruit-growers leave the mound, throwing up a little more earth each spring; others level off the ground in the fall after egg-laying has ceased. Before mounding, any larvæ already present should be cut out.

Copious applications of hot water to the base of the tree and roots (the covering earth having been removed) are usually effectual in destroying eggs or larvæ.

The bases of the trunks may be protected by covering with straw, as follows: "Scrape the earth away from the collar, place a handful of straight straw erect around the trunk, fastening it with twine; then return the soil, which will keep the ends of the straw in their places. The straw should entirely cover the bark, and the twine be loosed as the trunk increases in size."

Kansas Notes.—The pest is an American insect, unknown on the peach trees of other countries. It has been recognized in Kansas at least since 1873 (see E. A. Popenoe, Transactions Kansas State Horticultural Society 1873, p. 123).

OTHER INSECTS ATTACKING LARGE FRUITS.

ROCKY MOUNTAIN LOCUST.
INJURIOUS GRASSHOPPERS.
WHITE-MARKED TUSSOCK-MOTH — THE APPLE.
WALNUT MOTH.
BAG-WORM.

INSECTS ATTACKING SMALL FRUITS.

RASPBERRY SLUG.

(*Selandria rubi* Harris; Order, Hymenoptera.)

Diagnosis.—Infesting raspberries; dark-green, slug-like larvæ, about three-fourths of an inch long, feeding on the leaves, mostly during May; the coarse veins of the leaves are not eaten.

Description and Life-history.—The adult insect is a four-winged saw-fly, with transparent wings expanding about one-half of an inch. The veins of the wings are black. The front part of the body is black, the abdomen dark reddish. The adults appear soon after the young leaves are put forth, and insert their eggs beneath the skin of the raspberry leaf near the ribs and veins. The newly-hatched larva is small and whitish; as it grows older and larger it becomes green; the full-grown larva, or "slug," is from five-eighths to three-fourths of an inch long, dark green, with slightly yellowish tinge on the last two segments. A narrow, dark-green, longitudinal, dorsal line extends from the head to the last segment of the body. The head is bright, shining green. The body bears many small, branched spines, in length about one-fourth the diameter of the slug. It has 11 pairs of legs.

FIG. 51. RASPBERRY SLUG. *a*, larva; *b*, joints of larva, enlarged, to show arrangement of spiny hairs.

The larva is full-grown about June 1, and enters the ground, where it constructs a thin, tough cocoon of particles of earth fastened together by a sticky substance secreted by the larva. In this cocoon the larva quietly remains unchanged through the fall and winter, pupating in early spring, and emerging as the adult saw-fly about the middle of April.

Remedies.—Hand-picking is effective. White hellebore used as a powder (see p. 10) and dusted on the vines, or mixed with water — one ounce to two gallons of water — and sprayed on, is a successful remedy.

Kansas Notes.—In the crop report bulletin of the Kansas State Board of Agriculture for May, 1883, Prof. F. H. Snow treats of the pest. He says: "In the past three seasons I have noted the ravages of the larva of this insect upon the foliage of my neighbors' vines during the month of May. In some cases the number of worms were so great as to require constant watchfulness in order to prevent the entire defoliation of the vines."

STRAWBERRY LEAF-ROLLER.
(*Phoxopteris comptana* Froel.; Order, Lepidoptera.)

Diagnosis.—Attacking the strawberry; the leaves folded; their edges fastened together by silken cords, or the leaves crumpled and rolled into sub-cylindrical cases. Concealed in the fold, and feeding on the leaf in June, a small, brownish caterpillar, less than one-half an inch long, or a small chrysalis within the fold.

Attacking, also, the raspberry.

Description and Life-history.—The adult is a small, reddish-brown moth; expanse of wings about one-half an inch. The in-

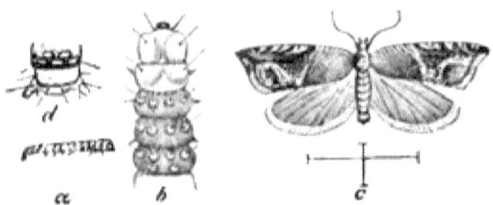

FIG. 52. STRAWBERRY LEAF-ROLLER; *a*, larva; *b*, back of front segments of larva, to show arrangement of hair-bearing tubercles; *d*, back of last segment of larva; *c*, adult.

sect is two-brooded in this latitude. The eggs for the first brood are laid in May, and the larvæ attain full development in June. About July 1 the bulk of the first-brood individuals are in chrysalis (they pupate within the folds of the leaves), and the adults soon appear. The eggs are soon laid, and by September 1 the voracious larvæ are capable of doing much damage. In the middle or latter part of this month the larvæ of this second brood are ready to pupate. They pass the winter in the pupal stage, the moths emerging the following spring.

The full-grown larva, which feeds upon the substance of the leaves, is from one-third to one-half an inch long, "and varies in color from yellowish-brown to green. The head is yellowish and horny with a dark, eye-like spot on each side. The second segment of the body has a shield above, colored and polished like the head, and on every segment there are a few pale dots, from each of which arises a single hair." The infested leaves look dry and scorched.

Remedies.—Because the larvæ are so effectively concealed in the folded leaves, spraying with arsenical mixtures is of little use. In new beds, where the plants are few in a row, the plants should be gone over carefully and the pests picked off and destroyed. In old beds the plants should be mowed off close to the ground while the insects of the first brood are in the pupal stage, *i. e.*, about July 1, and, after they have dried for a day or two, the patch should be burned over. This practice does not materially injure the roots of the plants, as they will immediately send out new sprouts. In the case of beds that are three or four years old, the best method is to plow them under and plant new ones. Avoid using plants from infested districts.

Kansas Notes.—The Strawberry Leaf-roller was first noticed in Kansas as an insect pest in 1880; it was noticeable also in 1881. In 1889 it was especially abundant. The pest is an imported one, and came to this country from Europe.

OTHER INSECTS ATTACKING SMALL FRUITS.

ROCKY MOUNTAIN LOCUST.
INJURIOUS GRASSHOPPERS.
TARNISHED PLANT-BUG.

INSECTS ATTACKING SHADE-TREES.

WHITE-MARKED TUSSOCK MOTH.
(*Orgyia leucostigma* Sm. and Abb.; Order. Lepidoptera.)

Diagnosis.—In late spring, and through the summer, handsome, hairy caterpillars about 1 inch to 1½ inches long, bright yellow, with bright red head, four cream-colored, brush-like tufts of hair on back, two rather long, black pencils of hair projecting forward from head end of body, and one black pencil projecting upward and backward from tail of body; feeding on maple, elm and other trees, and very noticeable crawling on sidewalks and fences close to shade-trees. All through the year cocoons on the trunks of trees, and on fences, walls of buildings, etc., near trees. Masses of eggs in brittle, shining, white substance fastened to bark or on cocoons.

Description and Life-history.—The adult insect is a moth; the female wingless, light gray, the oblong-oval body filled with eggs, and the moth usually found clinging to the outside of a cocoon;

FIG. 53. WHITE-MARKED TUSSOCK MOTH, larva.

the male is winged, the wings expanding about 1¼ inches, ashen-gray in color, with dark, wavy bands across the wings, and with beautifully feathered feelers or antennæ.

The insect passes the winter in the egg. The eggs are laid in masses, the eggs of each mass being held together and covered by a white, brittle, frothy-looking substance. The egg masses are rather conspicuous objects on tree trunks during the winter. In May and June the young larvæ appear, and begin eating the foliage of shade-trees. They are conspicuous because of their bright colors and striking bunches of hairs (see description of larva in Diagnosis). By the middle of July the larvæ are mostly full-grown, and spin silken cocoons, fastened to tree trunks, or to fences, walls of buildings, etc., near the trees. In these cocoons they pupate, and the adults soon appear. The adults of this brood are almost all out by August 1, at Lawrence. Eggs are soon laid, the females, on emerging from the cocoon, crawling upon its surface, and clinging there until the eggs are laid. They then die, and their withered bodies are often to be seen hanging on the cocoon. The eggs soon hatch, and before winter the brood has gone through its transformations and the eggs are laid, which pass through the winter, hatching the next May.

Remedies.—There are so many natural enemies of this pest, that it has much difficulty in maintaining its ground. Almost, if not quite, a dozen insect parasites have been found infesting it. In Lawrence, I have bred three ichneumon parasites from pupæ of this insect.

When it does become locally destructive, the egg masses should be picked off the tree trunks and fences in winter and destroyed.

Spraying infested trees with arsenicals (see p. 7) while the larvæ are young is effective.

Kansas Notes.—The White-marked Tussock Moth is well known in Kansas towns. However, it is noticeable that the large promise given by the first brood as to a probably overwhelming number of individuals of the second brood is rarely fulfilled, owing to the destructive work of the many parasites. From my notes on the occurrence of this pest in Lawrence last year, I quote as follows:

February 2.—Egg masses abundant on maples about town.

June 28.—Larvæ numerous; crawling on tree trunks, sidewalks, and fences; about one-half to three-fourths inch long.

July 15.—Very few larvæ now, most of them having spun cocoons and pupated. Many imagines have already emerged; and some eggs are laid. Noted several cocoons containing hymenopterous larvæ, parasitic. The cocoons are remarkably abundant on maple trees and in their vicinity. Fifty cocoons to a tree, on the lower 10 feet of trunk, is an average for an infested tree. Abundant along fences, on sides of houses and barns.

July 23.—The cocoons are badly infested by parasites. Most of the cocoons have given up the imagines and the females have laid their eggs, but the number of imagines is remarkably less than the number of cocoons spun up by the caterpillars.

The second brood of caterpillars was comparatively insignificant, owing to the effectiveness of the parasites.

WALNUT MOTH.

(*Datana angusii* G. & R.; Order, Lepidoptera.)

Diagnosis.—Infesting walnut and hickory; large, blackish caterpillars, feeding on the leaves; often large numbers, moulting, gathered in a mass or ball on the trunk or on large limbs; when feeding, remaining close together and entirely defoliating portions of the tree, often whole trees.

Description and Life-history.—The adult is a light-brown moth, with chestnut-brown head. There are several transverse, brown lines on the fore wings; the hind wings pale yellowish, unmarked. Expanse of wings about two inches.

The insect hibernates in the pupal stage in the ground. The moths emerge in June, and lay their eggs on the under surface of the walnut leaves. The larvæ, after hatching, keep together and

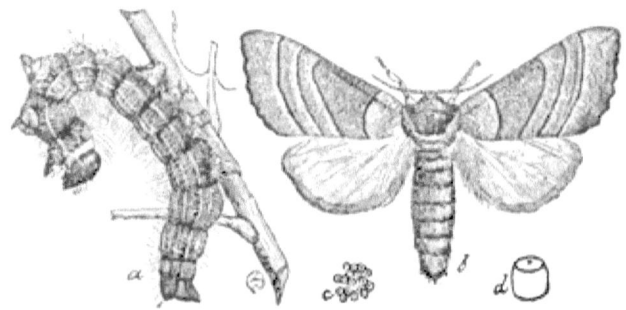

FIG. 54. YELLOW-NECKED APPLE-TREE CATERPILLAR (*Datana ministra*), closely allied to, and greatly resembling, the Walnut Moth (*Datana angusii*); *a*, larva; *b*, moth; *c*, eggs; *d*, an egg, greatly enlarged.

feed voraciously. They rapidly defoliate branches, and attract attention in this way. When ready to moult, they migrate in a body to some spot on the tree trunk, or on some large limb, and remain there in a solid, wriggling mass, until the skins have been cast. Returning to the leaves, they continue feeding. When full-grown, which they become in about five weeks, the caterpillar is entirely black, with scattering, long, whitish, wooly hairs over the body. When younger the color is rather wine-red. The larvæ descend from the tree at about the same time, and enter the ground, where they transform into naked, brown chrysalids. The moths emerge the following May or June.

Remedies.—Spraying the trees with London purple (see p. 8) or Paris green (see p. 7) while the caterpillars are young is effective; but it is as effective, and far easier, to capture the caterpillars when they come together to moult. The great, wriggling mass may be burned or crushed.

There are several parasitic flies which have the caterpillar at their mercy. I have watched a Tachinid fly industriously engaged in sealing the doom of many of the black larvæ.

This pest does not seem to be able to maintain itself in large numbers for several successive seasons. In fact, it is the exception to find it destructive in one locality for two successive seasons. Its very abundance the first season seems to give such numerical strength to its parasites as to practically exterminate it for the time being in that spot.

Kansas Notes.—In the Second Quarterly Report of the Kansas State Board of Agriculture for 1883 (December 31), Prof. F. H. Snow says that the Walnut Moth, "a hitherto almost unknown species of destructive caterpillar," appeared in large numbers in the month of August, 1883.

It was rather abundant in Lawrence in the summer of 1890, when it defoliated many walnut trees. It was hardly noticeable about the same trees in 1891.

BOX-ELDER BUG.

(*Leptocoris trivittatus* Say; Order. Hemiptera.)

Diagnosis.—Attacking the box-elder; a dull-black bug, about one-half inch long, with orange-red markings in lines; in large numbers on trunks of box-elder and other trees, or on sides of buildings. In winter the bugs frequent houses, and many appear in sunny places on warm days.

Attacking also ash, maple, and other shade-trees.

Description and Life-history.—The insect is a true sucking bug, getting its food by sucking the juice from plant foliage. It passes through the winter in the adult stage, the bugs seeking sheltered crevices and corners in stone walls, buildings, etc. In early spring they scatter to the trees, and lay their eggs in crevices in the bark and on the twigs. The young are soon hatched, and resemble the adults in general shape, but are of a nearly uniform red color. As they grow older, brownish and blackish colors begin to appear. The adult is thus described by Professor Popenoe:

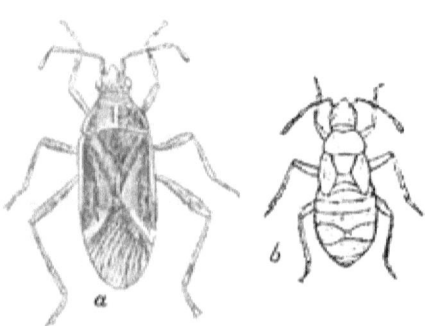

FIG. 55. BOX-ELDER BUG; *a*, adult; *b*, young.

Body about nine-sixteenths of an inch long, elongate-oval in outline, black, with red marks, to wit: Above, a median line and the lateral margins of the thorax, the anterior portion of the outside edges of the upper wings, and an oblique line separating the thicker, basal portion from the membranous terminal portion of each, red: below, three broad lines on the abdomen, two lateral and one median, and the globular basal joint of each leg, red; eyes brownish-red; antennæ slender, slightly thicker at tip, black; legs slender and, except the red basal joint, black.

The insects are harmless when swarming about the house in winter time, so far as attacking household effects goes. They have no jaws, and can only suck. However, they are disgusting and repulsive to the housewife, and are most unwelcome visitors.

Remedies.—When the bugs are assembled in large numbers, crushing or brushing into boiling water may be employed. Or kerosene (see p. 9), either pure or as an emulsion, may be applied by spraying or dashing with a broom. They cannot be killed by spraying the foliage with arsenicals, as they obtain their food from beneath the surface of the leaf.

Kansas Notes.—The life-history of this pest has been made known by the studies of Prof. E. A. Popenoe, of the State Agricultural College, at Manhattan. In the First Annual Report of the Kansas Experiment Station of the State Agricultural College, for the year 1888, Professor Popenoe (pp. 220–225) discusses the pest, and from this paper most of the foregoing notes have been taken.

In the Third Biennial Report of the State Board of Agriculture (1881–'82), Professor Popenoe refers briefly to the pest. The bug has been known at Manhattan as a tree pest since 1878. It may be seen in any part of the State now.

GREEN-STRIPED MAPLE-WORM.

(*Anisota rubicunda* Fabr.; Order, Lepidoptera.)

Diagnosis.—Attacking the maple; a naked caterpillar, about 1½ inches long, pale yellowish-green, longitudinally striped with lighter and darker green lines, two small, black horns on body behind the head; noticeable on the sidewalks.

Description and Life-history.—The adult insect is a beautiful, rosy-white moth, with wings expanding from 1½ to 2 inches. The eggs are laid in groups of 30 or more, on the under side of maple leaves, about the last of May. The larvæ or worms immediately on hatching begin their attacks on the maple's foliage, and feed about one month before becoming full-grown. They descend into the ground to pupate, and the adults appear in from 10 to 14 days. The insect is two-brooded, the first brood of worms appearing mostly in June, and the second late in July and early in August. The worms of the second brood are much more abundant than those of the first, and, consequently, the second brood is much more destructive. The larvæ enter the ground and pupate about September 1st. The chrysalids of this brood pass the winter in the ground, the moths emerging the following May.

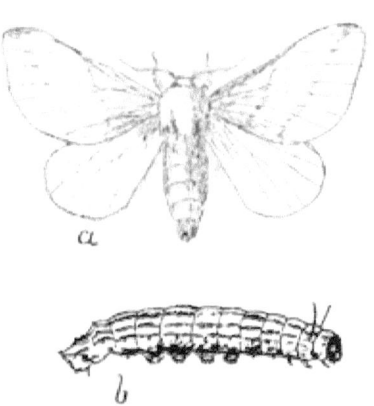

FIG. 56. GREEN-STRIPED MAPLE-WORM; *a*, adult; *b*, larva.

Remedies.—Several insect parasites attack the Maple-worm, much to the advantage of the maple tree. Several species of birds eagerly devour them also.

Spraying with London purple (see p. 8) or Paris green (see p. 7) early in the season, soon after the worms appear, will prove effective.

The worms when about to leave the trees may also be entrapped by digging a trench either around the individual tree or around a grove or belt. The trench should be at least a foot deep, with the outer wall slanting under. Great numbers of worms will collect in it, or bury themselves in its bottom, and may easily be killed.

Prof. F. H. Snow, in the Second Quarterly Report for 1883 (December), State Board of Agriculture, recommends the following remedial measures:

There are four opportunities presented in the life of each brood for the destruction of the species: The first is when the moths have just emerged from the chrysalis at the surface of the ground, and are helplessly crawling to some suitable spot for the drying of their slowly-expanding wings. They may easily be destroyed in this condition, and may be found in the greatest numbers between sundown and dark. The second opportunity is after the eggs have been deposited upon the lower surface of the leaves. The egg clusters may be detected and removed as already pointed out. The third opportunity is during the first week or 10 days of the little caterpillars' lives, before they have left the single leaf upon which the eggs were deposited. A whole colony may be removed by detaching the leaf. The fourth opportunity is when the caterpillars have reached their full growth, and are coming down the trunks of the trees to enter the ground for pupation. By improving these four opportunities for the destruction of the first brood, the second brood will require but little time and effort for its extinction, since but few individuals of the first brood will have escaped to become the parents of the second.

Kansas Notes.—Dr. Riley (Fifth Annual Report State Entomologist of Missouri, for 1872) records (p. 137 *et seq.*) the presence of this maple pest in Kansas. A correspondent in Franklin county (date, June 24, 1872) writes that he first observed the worms in his vicinity in 1870. He says:

. . . There were not a great many that year [1870], but last year [1871] they came in increased numbers, so that many trees were eaten bare, there not being a single leaf left. This year they are appearing by the million on the trees in my yard, and in fact on all the soft maples in this vicinity.

Dr. Riley says:

Anyone traveling through Kansas last fall [1872] must have been struck with the absolutely naked appearance of the soft maples, which are very extensively used, and highly prized for ornament and shade, and may be found in every thrifty town.

Mr. G. C. Brackett, in the Transactions State Horticultural Society for 1873, refers to the Maple-worm as follows:

Thousands of trees during the past summer, in my section, ornamenting the roads, skirting our farms, adorning our door-yards, were completely stripped of every leaf; and what is most to be feared (as has been reported in other States) is, that as their numbers become so great that, having devoured the leaves on the maples, they will begin upon our orchards and other varieties of trees.

In 1874 the ravages of the pest were more extended, and in 1875, according to Professor Snow (Second Quarterly Report for 1883, State Board of Agriculture), nearly every maple in the city of Lawrence was entirely deprived of its foliage by the second brood of caterpillars, before the end of August. Continuing, Professor Snow says:

This same condition of affairs existed in nearly every town of eastern Kansas. It was hoped that after a year or two this insect, as is the habit of the species in the Eastern States, would disappear from notice. But it has continued its depredations for 11 continuous seasons with varying pertinacity, but in every year to such an extent as to produce complete defoliation of the maples in many localities.

Professor Snow noted the following birds feeding upon the worms: Robin, blue-bird, tufted titmouse, yellow-billed cuckoo, red-headed woodpecker, red-eyed vireo, and crow black-bird.

BAG-WORM.

(*Thyridopteryx ephemeræformis* Haworth; Order, Lepidoptera.)

Diagnosis.—Attacking evergreen trees; caterpillars inclosed in cases or bags, with head and front body with six legs projecting; feeding on various trees, especially evergreens. The cases are silken, and covered with bits of leaves or twigs or pine needles. In winter the cases, bags or baskets hang in the trees and contain eggs.

Attacking, also, various deciduous trees, as the elm, maple, locust, apple, pear, plum, cherry, peach, and quince.

Description and Life-history.—The adult insect is a moth, the female wingless, the male with four transparent wings, body black. The larvæ hatch in May and June, from eggs which have passed the winter in hanging cases. The young larvæ immediately make coverings of silk, the bags, for themselves, which they enlarge as their bodies grow. The silken cases are covered without with bits of leaves or twigs, rendering them hard to distinguish from the foliage of the tree. When the larva is feeding or traveling, the head and front end of the body, with the six legs, project from the bag. The projecting part of the body of the larva is rather horny, and is mottled with black and white; that part of the body within the bag is soft, and dull, brownish-red.

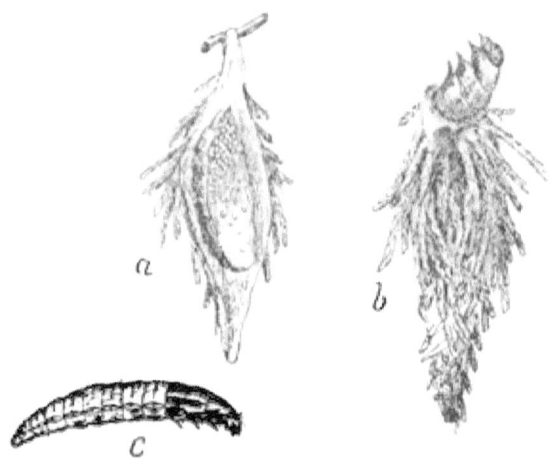

FIG. 57. BAG-WORM; a, case cut open, containing eggs; b, larva in case; c, larva.

When ready to pupate, the larva fastens the bag securely to some limb and changes within the case. The female moth on hatching does not leave the bag, but awaits the male near the entrance to the case. She lays her eggs within the bag, and then drops out of it to the ground and dies. The eggs hatch the following year.

The injury to the foliage is done, of course, by the larva while feeding. The pest appears to prefer coniferous to deciduous trees.

Remedies.—There are several parasitic insects which do much to keep the Bag-worm in check.

Gathering the cases, which contain the eggs, in winter is a sure remedy.

Spraying the foliage of infested trees with London purple (see p. 8) or Paris green (see p. 7) in the early summer, while the worms are young, will be effective.

As the female is wingless, the spread of this pest is slow; and if one rids his premises of the insect, he will not have all his labor brought to naught by the indifference of some neighbor, as can more easily happen in the case of other insect pests.

Kansas Notes.—The Bag-worm has been known for several

years as a shade-tree pest; it has not occurred in alarming numbers at any time, however, and its occurrence is largely local in character.

A correspondent in Sedgwick county reported that in August, 1891, he gathered at least a half-bushel of bags from a single tree, an Irish juniper.

OTHER INSECTS ATTACKING SHADE-TREES.

ROCKY MOUNTAIN LOCUST.
INJURIOUS GRASSHOPPERS.
FALL WEB-WORM.

INSECTS ATTACKING FLOWERS.

RED SPIDER.
(*Tetranychus telarius* Linn.; Order, Acarina.)

Diagnosis.—A minute, red mite on lower surface of leaves of house plants, spinning fine webs; the leaves turning yellow, withering, and falling off.

Description and Life-history.—The "Red Spider" is not a spider, but a mite, belonging to the same insect order as the flour and cheese mites (which are white instead of red).

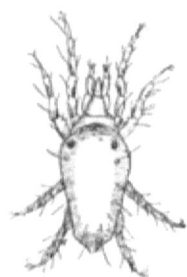

FIG. 58. RED SPIDER, greatly enlarged.

Under a microscope, (for the Red Spider is so small as to appear to the naked eye merely as a fine, red speck,) the little pest will be seen to have four pairs of legs, and to have mouth-parts fitted for piercing and sucking. The mite inserts its tiny beak into the leaf and sucks the life juices from the plant. The mites are usually in small colonies, under a fine, transparent web.

Remedies.—The Red Spider does not like a damp atmosphere; if the plants are well watered daily, our little pest will be seriously discouraged.

Spraying the plants with soap-suds, tobacco water, or kerosene emulsion (see p. 9), the last being best of all, will effectually keep the Red Spider down.

Kansas Notes.—Kansas housewives have been troubled by this pest whenever and wherever they have attempted to beautify their homes with the presence of flowers.

ROSE SLUG.
(*Selandria rosæ* Harr.; Order, Hymenoptera.)

Diagnosis.—A soft, greenish or yellowish, slug-like worm, about one-half an inch long, eating large, irregular patches in the upper surface of rose leaves; the leaves appear as if scorched, and drop off.

Description and Life-history.—(For illustration see Fig. 51, which shows the Raspberry Slug, a closely-allied form.) The adult insect is a four-winged fly, belonging to the family of saw-flies, in the same order with the ants, bees, and wasps. Its wings are transparent, and expand about one-half of an inch. The body is blackish.

The eggs are laid under the skin of the rose leaf (the saw-flies are so named because the females have a peculiar, saw-like, egg-laying apparatus, by means of which the eggs are laid in small incisions in the food-plant), and the larvæ, or young slugs, hatch in about two weeks.

The larvæ are not full-grown until about three weeks have passed, during which time they feed voraciously on the leaves. The slug has a small, yellowish head, with a black dot on each side of it, and has 11 pairs of short legs. When young, the body is semi-transparent and green; when older, the body is more opaque and has a yellowish color. The skin of the back is wrinkled, and covered with minute points. In feeding, they do not eat entirely through the leaf, but leave the veins and lower skin intact, eating only the upper surface. The leaves are, of course, killed, and a badly-infested rose-bush appears as if scorched by fire. The feeding is done mostly by night and on dark days; at other times the slugs rest on the under side of the leaves.

When the larvæ are full-grown they drop to the ground, dig into it, and pupate within a silk-lined cell. They emerge as adults the following spring.

Remedies.—White hellebore (see p. 10) or pyrethrum (see p. 9) may be dusted on the leaves, or may be sprayed on. Use two tablespoonfuls of white hellebore to a bucket of water. If the insecticides are to be dusted on, choose a time when the leaves are damp with dew.

Mr. Garman, entomologist at the Kentucky State College, has used London purple (see p. 8) and Paris green (see p. 7) with good effect. He used one pound of the dry poison to 100 gallons of water. These poisons cannot be sprayed on the bushes after the flower-buds unfold without destroying the petals.

Kansas Notes.—This pest is well known in rose gardens throughout the State.

NOXIOUS INSECTS OF THE HOUSEHOLD.

COCKROACHES.

(*Periplaneta orientalis* Linn. and *Blatta germanica* Stephens; Order, Orthoptera.)

Diagnosis.—Black, flattened, soft-bodied insects, in damp places about the home; in the kitchen and laundry especially.

Description and Life-history.—The common Cockroaches of the house are imported species, being natives of Asia and Europe. When full-grown, they are about two-thirds of an inch long. The eggs are laid in small packets, and the young roaches resemble the adults, except that they are smaller and lighter in color. The roaches attack provisions of all kinds; are almost omnivorous, in fact. They feed at night, retiring during the day-time into crevices and corners.

FIG. 59. COCKROACH (*Blatta germanica*.)

Remedies.—Pyrethrum (see p. 9) can be used against these pests with good effect. Dr. Riley says:

Just before nightfall, go into the infested rooms and puff it into all crevices, under base boards, into drawers and cracks of old furniture—in fact, wherever there is a crack—and in the morning the floor will be covered with dead and dying, or demoralized and paralyzed, roaches, which may easily be swept up or otherwise collected and burned. With cleanliness, and persistency in these methods, the pest may be substantially driven out of the house, and should never be allowed to get full possession by immigrants from without.

Kansas Notes.—Common, and often seriously troublesome, throughout the State.

BUFFALO BEETLE.

(*Anthrenus scrophulariæ* Linn.; Order, Coleoptera.)

Diagnosis.—Small, dark-colored, hairy creatures, infesting carpets; hiding in cracks and crevices about the house; known to housekeepers as "fish moths," "buffalo moths," etc.

Description and Life-history.—The adult insect is a small beetle, not a moth, about a quarter of an inch long, black with white spots, and with an irregular red stripe along the back. The beetles begin to appear in the fall, and continue to appear through the winter and spring. The beetles may often be seen in the windows. They fly out-of-doors, and are found on flowers of the orders Compositæ and Scrophulariaceæ.

The eggs are laid soon after the appearance of the beetles, probably upon the carpets. The eggs are soon hatched, and the destructive larvæ begin to feed upon the carpets, stored woolen goods,

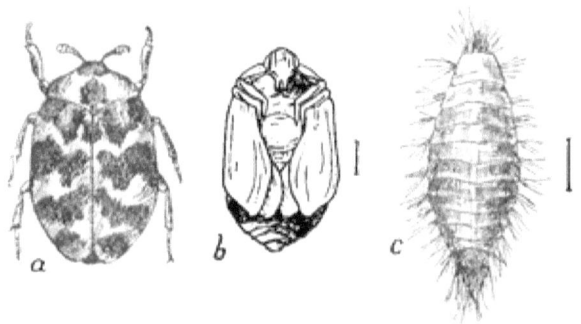

FIG. 60. BUFFALO BEETLE: *a*, adult beetle (natural length about one-fourth inch); *b*, pupa; *c*, larva.

or furs. They moult several times (the cast skins may often be found), and when full-grown the larva seeks a sheltered place and transforms into the quiescent pupa, which later becomes the perfect beetle.

It is in the larval state, of course, that the damage to the carpets is done. The full-grown larva is about one-third of an inch in length. It "is brown in color, and clothed with stiff, brown hairs, which are longer around the sides than on the back, and still longer at the extremities. Both at sides and extremities they form tufts, the hinder end being furnished with three tufts of long hair, and the head with a dense bunch of shorter hair."

Remedies.—Rugs which are often taken up and shaken do not offer suitable dwelling-places for the pest. When carpets are used, and only taken up once a year, the Buffalo Beetle finds a secure haven, and rejoices accordingly.

At house-cleaning time, carpets should be removed at the same time from as many rooms as possible, the rooms thoroughly cleaned, and benzine carefully puffed with a hand-atomizer into all cracks and crevices in the floor; particular attention should be given the base boards. In addition, it would be advisable to fill the floor cracks with a mixture of plaster of Paris and water, which, on setting, will leave no convenient homes of refuge for the pest. Around the borders of the room a width of tarred paper should be laid, and the carpets, which should have been thoroughly beaten, lightly sprayed with benzine, and aired, then relaid.

Dr. Riley says that in a room so cleaned the pest will probably be unable to gain a foot-hold during the ensuing year.

Dr. Riley recommends, for times other than house cleaning, the laying of a damp cloth over suspected places in the carpet, and ironing it with a hot iron. The steam thus generated will pass through the carpet and kill all the insects immediately beneath. Hot water poured along the edges of the carpets is recommended.

If the pests are in furniture or clothing, they may be killed by spraying with benzine or gasoline. Remember that these substances are highly inflammable.

CLOTHES-MOTH.

(*Tinea pellionella* Linn.; Order, Lepidoptera.)

Diagnosis.—A number of small, cylindrical rolls or cases, in each of which is a small, white, soft-bodied grub (larva); feeding on woolens, hair-cloth, fur, or feathers.

Description and Life-history.—The adult insect is a very small, light-brown moth, the wings expanding about one-third of an inch. They begin to appear in May, and are to be seen through the summer. The eggs are laid on garments hanging in closets and wardrobes, on stored furs, feathers, etc. The larvæ, immediately on hatching, make small, cylindrical rolls or cases from bits of the cloth or fur upon which they are feeding. The larva is about three-sixteenths of an inch long, white, soft-bodied, with eight pairs of legs, and continues its destructive attacks during the summer and fall. Late in the fall it closes the ends of its

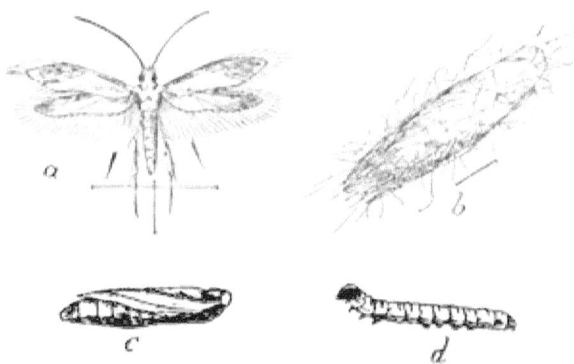

FIG. 61. CLOTHES-MOTH; *a*, adult; *b*, case enclosing larva; *c*, pupa; *d*, larva. (The natural lengths of larva and pupa approximate the line at the side of the *b*, the case.

case, and lies torpid through the winter. In spring it pupates within the case, and issues as the adult moth in May or later. The insect in all of its stages is easily distinguished from the "buffalo moth," which as an adult is a beetle, and which as a larva does not live within a case.

Remedies.—Dr. Riley's suggestions for combating this household pest are as follows:

During the latter part of May, or early in June, a vigorous campaign should be entered upon. All carpets, cloth-covered furniture, furs and rugs should be thoroughly shaken and aired, and, if possible, exposed to sunlight as long as practicable. If the house is badly infested, or if any particular article is supposed to be badly infested, a free use of benzine, in the manner mentioned in my last article [as in case of Buffalo Beetle, see page 110], will be advisable. All floor cracks and dark closets should be sprayed with this substance. Too much pains cannot be taken to destroy every moth and every egg and every newly-hatched larva, for immunity for the rest of the year depends largely, almost entirely, upon the thoroughness with which the work of extermination is carried on at this time. The benzine spray will kill the insect in every stage, and it is one of the few substances which will destroy the egg. I would, however, repeat the caution as to its inflammability. No light should be brought into a room in which it has been used until after a thorough airing, and until the odor is almost dissipated.

The proper packing away of furs and winter clothing through the summer is a serious matter. A great deal of unnecessary expenditure in the way of cedar chests and cedar wardrobes, and various compounds in the way of powders, has been urged by writers on these pests. But experience fully proves that, after a thorough treatment in May or June, garments may be safely put away for the rest of the season with no other protection than wrapping them closely in stout paper, to preclude infection through some belated female.

Cloth-covered furniture which is in constant use will not be harmed, and the same may be said of cloth-lined carriages. Where such furniture is stored away or kept unused in a dark room, or where the carriages are left in a dark coach-house through the summer, at least two sprayings with benzine, say once in June and once about August 1st, will be advisable. Another plan which will act as a protection in such cases is to sponge the cloth linings and covers, on both sides where possible, with a dilute solution of corrosive sublimate in alcohol, made just strong enough not to leave a white mark on a black feather.

Kansas Notes.—An imported pest, common all over the United States.

ANTS.

(Family, *Formicidæ;* Order, Hymenoptera.)

Diagnosis.—Ants in greater or lesser numbers infesting the house.

Description and Life-history.—Ants are too familiar to require describing. They have strong jaws, which they use effectively. They belong to the so-called "social insects," and large numbers live together in one nest. The eggs and young are cared for by the adult workers. The young are helpless, footless grubs; in the pupal stage they are popularly known as "ant eggs," being inclosed at this time in little, white cases, which are frequently to be seen being carried about by the adults. Long lines of workers, extending from food-supply to nest, are often seen, the ants passing to and fro, and carrying particles of food to the nest. If many nests are established in a house, the foraging ants quite overrun the premises.

Remedies.—The best remedies are those applied to the nests. By careful hunting, tracing up lines of ants, following food-carrying workers, etc., the nests may be found, and if they can then be reached, hot water, benzine (see p. 10) or bisulphide of carbon (see p. 10) may be applied, killing young and old. Care should be exercised in using inflammable substances, as benzine and bisulphide of carbon.

APPENDIX.

THE HORN FLY OF CATTLE.

(*Hæmatobia serrata* R.-Desv.; Order, Diptera.)

This cattle pest has not yet made its way into Kansas [*] (at least, is so far unnoticed here,) but its appearance in Illinois this summer, (Dr. Williston, on August 25, received specimens from Mr. John Marten, Champaign, Ill., Assistant State Entomologist,) and its steady migration westward, induces me to append here a brief account of its habits, etc. The Horn Fly in America has been studied independently by Prof. J. B. Smith, and by Mr. L. O. Howard and Mr. C. L. Marlatt, of the division of entomology, United States Department of Agriculture, under the direction of Dr. C. V. Riley, chief of the division, and their observations have been recorded in Insect Life, vol. II, No. 4, (October, 1889,) pp. 93-103. From this account the following brief notes are chiefly taken.

Diagnosis.—Attacking cattle; swarms of small, black flies in summer, gathered, when feeding, "over the back and flanks and on the legs" of cattle, sucking the blood. When resting, the flies, if abundant, cluster around the bases of the horns (whence the name). To distinguish the Horn Fly from other cattle-infesting flies, note the habit of clustering on the horns, and compare specimens with the description. See "Description and Life-history" to follow.

Description and Life-history.—The fly is about one-sixth of an inch long, black, with brownish and grayish tinges. Wings

---

[*] Since writing this (September), an article on "the Cow-horn Fly," by Prof. E. A. Popenoe, of the Kansas State Agricultural College, Manhattan, appeared in the *Industrialist*, October 8, in which the author states that the fly has appeared in Kansas. He says:

"So far as recorded, Manhattan is the westernmost point yet reached by this fly, and it has been noticed here only since the 19th of September last, when it was observed by Assistant Marlatt on milch cows a mile from the college. Since that date it has been found on various herds in this immediate vicinity, but is apparently yet restricted to a narrow area, herds a few miles away showing no evidence of its presence."

A newspaper account of the appearance of a "small black fly" in "great numbers," infesting cattle about Guthrie, O. T., these flies gathering in clusters on the bases of the horns, leads me to suspect the presence of this pest among the cattle of the Indian Territory.

sub-transparent, with slightly blackish tinge, but with no spots or markings other than the veins. The flies first appear in May (in Virginia), and remain until "right cold weather." They attack the cattle in the fields, probably never penetrating the stables (Raillict).

When on the cattle and sucking the blood, the wings are slightly elevated and are held out from the body, not at right angles, but approaching it—approximately an angle of 60° from the abdomen. The legs are spread out widely, and the beak inserted beneath the skin of the animal, and is held in nearly a perpendicular position. . . . The fly, before inserting its beak, has worked its way through the hairs, close to the skin. While feeding, however, the hairs, which can be seen over its body, do not seem to interfere with its speedy flight when alarmed; for at a fling of the tail, or an impatient turn of the head, the flies rise instantly in a cloud for a foot or two, returning again as quickly and resuming their former positions.

When the flies are abundant, the characteristic habit of clustering about the bases of the horns is indulged in. They do no damage at all to the horns; the popular notions that the fly eats into the substance of the horns, causes them to rot, and lays eggs in them from which maggots hatch which penetrate into the brain, are all without foundation of fact. The flies congregate on the horns solely for rest in a place where they may be undisturbed. The resting position of the flies differs from the sucking position, in that while on the horn the wings are held nearly flat down the back, overlapping at base, and diverging only moderately at tip. The beak is held in a nearly horizontal position, and the legs are not widely spread.

When feeding, the flies are found over the back and flanks and on the legs. During a rain storm, they flock beneath the belly. When the animal is lying down, a favorite place of attack seems to be under the thigh and back belly, around the bag. On the horns, the flies form clusters entirely around the horn for a space of two inches from the base; they seem to prefer the concave to the convex side of the horn.

The eggs are laid by the flies in freshly-dropped dung, in the day-time, and are laid singly, never in clusters. The larvæ issue within twenty-four hours after the eggs have been laid, and descend into the dung, not very deep. The larvæ are dirty-white maggots, not more than one-third of an inch long. The larvæ become fully grown in about five days, and descend into the ground below the dung from a half to three-quarters of an inch to pupate. The adult flies issue from the pupariæ in about one week, so that two weeks is about the average time from the laying of the egg to the appearance of the flies. "With four active breeding months, May 15 to September 15, there will be eight generations," so that the large numbers of the flies are not surprising.

Of the amount of damage done by the fly, Messrs. Riley and Howard (Insect Life, *loc. cit.*) say:

> The amount of damage done by the fly has been exaggerated by some, and underestimated by others. We have heard many rumors of the death of animals from its attacks, but have been unable to substantiate a single case. We believe that the flies alone will never cause the death of an animal. They reduce the condition of stock to a considerable extent, and, in the case of milch cows, the yield of milk is reduced from one-fourth to one-half. It is our opinion that their bites seldom produce sores by themselves, although we have seen a number of cases where large sores had been made by the cattle rubbing themselves against trees and fences, in an endeavor to allay the irritation caused by the bites; or, in spots where they could not rub, by licking constantly with the tongue, as about the bag and on the inside of the hind thighs. A sore once started in this way will increase with the continued irritation by the flies, and will be difficult to heal. Those who underestimate the damage believe that the flies do not suck blood; but such persons have doubtless watched the flies only upon the horns or elsewhere, in their resting position, when the beak is not inserted, or have caught them and crushed them when their bodies contained little blood. In reality, the flies suck a considerable amount of blood, however, and it is their only nourishment; if captured and crushed at the right time, the most skeptical individual will be convinced.

Remedies.—The following notes on remedial measures are quoted from Insect Life (*loc. cit.*):

> PREVENTIVE APPLICATIONS.—Almost any greasy substance will keep the flies away for several days. A number of experiments were tried in the field, with the result that train-oil alone, and train-oil with a little sulphur or carbolic acid added, will keep the flies away for from five to six days, while, with a small proportion of carbolic acid, it will have a healing effect upon the sores which may have formed. Train-oil should not cost more than 50 to 75 cents per gallon, and a gallon will anoint a number of animals. Common axle grease, costing 10 cents per box, will answer nearly as well, and this substance has been extensively and successfully used by Mr. William Johnson, a large stock dealer at Warrenton, Va. Tallow has also been used to good advantage. The practice of smearing the horns with pine or coal tar simply repels them from these parts. Train-oil or fish-oil seems to be more lasting in its affects than any other of the substances used.

APPLICATIONS TO DESTROY THE FLY.—A great deal has been said during the summer concerning the merits of a proprietary substance, consisting mainly of tobacco dust and creosote, known as "X. O. Dust," and manufactured by a Baltimore firm, as an application to cattle, and it has received an indorsement from Prof. J. B. Smith, entomologist of the New Jersey Experiment Station. We are convinced that this substance has considerable merit as an insecticide, and know from experience that it will kill many of the flies when it touches them, although they die slowly, and a few may recover. The substance costs 25 cents a pound, and is not lasting in its effects. Where it is dusted through the hair, the flies on alighting will not remain long enough to bite, but two days later, according to our experience, they are again present in as great numbers as before. A spray of kerosene emulsion directed upon a cow would kill the flies quite as surely, and would be cheaper, but we do not advise an attempt to reduce the number of the pests by actually killing the flies.

HOW TO DESTROY THE EARLY STAGES.—Throwing a spadeful of lime upon a cow-dung will destroy the larvæ which are living in it, and as in almost every pasture there are some one or two spots where the cattle preferably congregate during the heat of the day, the dung which contains most of the larvæ will, consequently, be more or less together, and easy to treat at once. If the evil should increase, therefore, it will well pay a stock raiser to start a load of lime through his field occasionally, particularly in May or June, as every larva killed then represents the death of very many flies during August. We feel certain that this course will be found in many cases practical and of great avail, and will often be of great advantage to the pasture, besides.

Kansas Notes.—The Horn Fly occurs in France, and perhaps elsewhere in Europe. It was first noted in America in 1887. Dr. S. W. Williston, in an article entitled "A New Cattle Pest," *American Naturalist*, vol. XXIII, p. 584, says:

On October 5, 1887, I received from Professor Cope specimens of a fly taken from the cattle of Mr. Thomas Sharpless, of West Chester, Pa., with the information, shortly afterward, that the flies had been observed during the year at that place in small swarms. . . . The flies, I was also told, were observed the same year on the land of Mr. George Pim, of Marshallton, Chester county. I am thus particular in giving the facts as told to me, for this is the first record, of which I am aware, of the introduction from Europe of a cattle pest that bids fair to extend itself over the whole United States, and be as troublesome as its nearly related pest, the well-known Stable Fly, or Cattle Fly, also European originally. *Stomoxys calcitrans* Linn.

In September, 1887, specimens were sent to Dr. Riley from Camden, N. J. The following year the pest was reported from the same place, and also from Harford, Md.

By the summer of 1889 the pest had extended in numbers much farther to the southward, and the Department [of Agriculture] was early informed of its occurrence in Harford and Howard counties, Maryland, and Prince William, Fanquier, Stafford, Culpepper, Louisa, Augusta, Buckingham and Bedford counties, Virginia. Other scattering observations show the migration southward and westward of the pest.

Prof. Herbert Osborn, in Bulletin 13, Iowa Agricultural Experiment Station, May, 1891, says:

. . . It is becoming distributed throughout the country. It will doubtless appear in this State in the near future, though at present writing, except for one uncertain statement as to its appearance in the southeast part of the State, I have seen no report of its occurrence in Iowa.

At the third annual meeting of the American Association of Economic Entomologists, held in August, 1891, Mr. D. S. Kellicott, of Columbus, Ohio, stated that the Horn Fly certainly has a foot-hold in central Ohio. He thought the fly was advancing along the Baltimore & Ohio Railway, and spreading south from Lancaster, a village near this railroad line. Mr. Lintner, State Entomologist of New York, at the same time said that he had heard of the fly in the southeastern portion of New York State. In Insect Life, vol. II, p. 144 (1890), P. T. Henshaw, under date of August 20, reports the presence of the Horn Fly in Kentucky. He says that the flies have been numerous all summer. P. H. Rolfs reports the pest in Florida in 1891 (Insect Life, vol. IV, p. 398, 1892). In Insect Life, vol. IV (April, 1892), the presence of the pest in Mississippi is reported by Howard Evarts Weed, a competent entomologist. He says it was noticed in his State in May, 1891, and on inquiry he found that the insect was "present in nearly all of the eastern portions of the State." Referring to the probable destruction and abundance of the pest, Mr. Weed says:

. . . It seems to me probable that it will eventually become a more serious pest in the Southern than in the Northern States."

It will be of interest to note the first appearance of the pest in Kansas.* Its appearance in Illinois (see note at the beginning of the Appendix) makes it highly probable that the coming season will find it within the borders of our State.

---

*See foot-note on page 113. One is led to reflect upon the increasing value of economic entomology as its number of observers grows larger, and it becomes possible to hoist warning flags in front of the destructive insect waves.

INDEX.

[The page references in italic figures indicate the page where the principal discussion of the insect begins.]

	PAGE.
Acrididæ	41
Ægeria exitiosa Say	91
Allen county	34, 77
American Naturalist	116
Amphicerus bicaudatus Say	81
Anasa tristis De Geer	56
Anderson county	18, 19, 40, 77
Angoumois Grain Moth	50, 52, 53
Anisopteryx vernata Peck	75
Anisota rubicunda Fabr	101
Anthrenus scrophulariæ Linn	109
Ants	112
Aphis maidi-radicis Forbes	20
Aphis maidis Fitch	21
Appendix A	113
Apple, insects attacking	67, 69, 73, 75, 78, 80, 81, 83, 85, 92, 103
Apple-root Louse	73
Apple-tree Borer	4, 7
Apple-tree Tent Caterpillar	84, 85
Apple-tree Twig Borer	81
Arsenic, not absorbed by plants	12
Ashby, G. W.	73
Ash, insects attacking	99
Atchison county	34
Bag-worm	3, 103
Bag-worm, attacking large fruits	92
Barton county	37
Basket-worm — see Bag-worm.	
Bean, insects attacking	63
Bean Weevil	4, 63
Beckwith, M. B.	11
Benzine	10
Bisulphide of carbon	10
Biting insects	1
Blatta germanica Stephens	108
Blissus leucopterus Say	13
Borers — see Flat-headed Apple-tree Borer, Round-headed Apple-tree Borer, Apple-twig Borer.	
Bourbon county	19
Box-elder Bug	99
Box-elder, insects attacking	99
Brown county	21, 34

(119)

Bruchus obtectus Say	64
Bruchus pisi Linn	62
Brackett, G. C.	67, 69, 73, 75, 77, 84, 86, 88, 102
Buffalo Beetle	109
Buffalo Moth — see Buffalo Beetle.	
Bulach	9
Bulletin of Iowa Agricultural Experiment Station	117
Bulletin of Kansas State Board of Agriculture	94
Butler county	34
Cabbage, insects attacking	57, 59, 60, 61
Cabbage Plusia	61
Cabbage-worm — see Imported Cabbage-worm, Southern Cabbage-worm.	
Calandria sp.	52
Carbolic acid	10
Carpets, insects infesting	109
Carpocapsa pomonella Linn	78
Cassida sp	55
Caterpillar, definition	3
Cattle Fly (*Stomoxys calcitrans* Linn.)	116
Cattle, insects attacking	113
Cecidomyia destructor Say	29
Cereal crops, insects attacking	13, 28, 29, 40
Cereals, other than corn and wheat, insects attacking	41, 49
Chase county	34
Chautauqua county	34, 77
Cherokee county	34
Cherry Aphis	90
Cherry, insects attacking	80, 90, 103
Cheyletus sp., attacking Flax-seed Mite	53
Chinch-bug	1, 2, 5, 13, 33, 49
Chinch-bug, attacking grasses and cereals other than corn and wheat	49
Chinch-bug, attacking wheat	40
Chrysalid, definition of	4
Chrysobothris femorata Fabr	69
Chrysomelidæ	17
Clark county	26
Clay county	34
Clisiocampa americana Harris	85
Cloud county	34
Clothes-moth	110
Clothes-moth Worm	3
Cockroaches	108
Codlin Moth	1, 3, 69, 78
Coffey county	34, 77
Conotrachelus nenuphar Herbst	87, 89
Contagious disease of Chinch-bug	14
Contagious disease of Chinch-bug, how to obtain and use infected bugs	15
Cope, E. D.	116
Coptocycla sp	55
Corn, insects attacking	13, 28
Corn-louse	20, 21
Corn-root Louse	20
Corn-root Worm	7
Corn Worm	27
Corn Worm, attacking the tomato	66
Cowley county	26, 34
Crawford county	34
Cucumber Beetle	4, 7, 65
Cucumber, insects attacking	65

INDEX.

Curculio — see Plum Curculio.	
Dalmatian insect powder.........	9
Datana angusii G. and R........	98
Davis county.............................34, 38,	39
Davis, John........................	39
Deming, N. P......................	75
Diabrotica longicornis Say.........	17
Diabrotica 12-punctata Oliv........	19
Diabrotica vittata Fabr............	65
Diagnosis, what it is...............	6
Dickinson county..................34,	38
Differential Locust.................	42
Dissosteira longipennis Thomas.....	43
Division of Entomology U. S. Department of Agriculture, Bulletin of........44, 47,	48
Doniphan county...................	34
Douglas county...................34, 38, 40, 53, 62, 66, 77, 86, 97, 99,	103
Doyle, D...........................	91
Elk county.......................34,	77
Ellis county........................	34
Ellsworth county..................34,	37
Elm, insects attacking.............	103
Empusa aphidis Hoffm.............	15
Empusa aphidis, parasitic on Grasshopper.	48
Entomopthora sp., on Grasshoppers..	48
Eupelmus allyni, parasite on Wheat-straw Worm..	36
Eurycreon rantalis Guenée........	25
Evergreen trees, insects attacking...	103
Experiment Station, Kansas State Agricultural College....	64
Fall Army-worm...................3,	39
Fall Army-worm, attacking corn.....	28
Fall Army-worm, attacking garden crops..	66
Fall Army-worm, attacking grasses and cereals other than corn and wheat.....	49
Fall Web-worm..................3,	83
Fall Web-worm, attacking shade-trees.	105
Feathers, insects attacking.........	110
Finney county...................47, 48,	49
Fish-oil soap.......................	10
Fish Moth — see Buffalo Beetle.	
Flat-headed Apple-tree Borer.......69,	75
Flax-seed Mite.....................	53
Fletcher, J.....................8, 10, 11,	12
Flowers, insects attacking..........	106
Forbes, S. A...................16, 20, 29, 32,	60
Formicidæ........................	112
Franklin county..................34, 75,	102
Fruits, large, insects attacking......67,	92
Fruits, small, insects attacking......93,	95
Furs, insects attacking..............	110
Garden crops, insects attacking.....55,	66
Garden Web-worm................3,	25
Garden Web-worm, attacking garden crops..	66
Garden Web-worm, attacking grasses and cereals other than corn and wheat.....	49
Garman, H. A......................	107
Gasoline...........................	10
Gas-tar............................	10
Gelechia cerealiella Oliv...........	50
Gibbs, George.....................	46
Gillette, C. P......................	8
Glover, Townend..................	16

INDEX.

Godfrey, A. N.	59, 83, 85
Grain Moth — see Angoumois Grain Moth.	
Grain Weevils	52
Grasses, attacked by Chinch-bug	13
Grasses, insects attacking	41, 49
Grasshoppers — see Injurious Grasshoppers.	
Greeley county	49
Green-striped Maple-worm	101
Greenwood county	59
Grub, definition of	3
Harmotobia serrata R. Desv	113
Hamilton county	47, 49
Harlequin Cabbage Bug	57
Harper county	34
Harvey county	34
Heliothis armigera Hübner	27
Hellebore	10
Henshaw, P. T	117
Hessian Fly	1, 7, 29, 37
Hickory, insects attacking	98
Hopper-dozer	46
Horn Fly of Cattle	113
Horse-radish, insects attacking	57
Household, insects infesting the	108
Houston, D. W	77
Howard, L. O	113, 115
Hull, E. S	88
Hunter, S. J	18, 19
Hyphantria textor Harris	83
Imported Cabbage-worm	59, 60, 61, 62
Industrialist	113
Injurious Grasshoppers	7, 24, 25, 41
Injurious Grasshoppers, attacking corn	28
Injurious Grasshoppers, attacking garden crops	66
Injurious Grasshoppers, attacking grasses and cereals other than corn and wheat	49
Injurious Grasshoppers, attacking large fruits	92
Injurious Grasshoppers, attacking shade-trees	105
Injurious Grasshoppers, attacking small fruits	95
Injurious Grasshoppers, attacking wheat	40
Insecticides	7
Insect Life	16, 54, 64, 113, 115, 117
Introduction	1
Iowa Agricultural Experiment Station, Bulletins	117
Isosoma tritici Riley	35
Jackson county	34
Jefferson county	34, 40
Johnson county	18, 33, 34
Johnson, G. Y.	86
Johnson, Wm	115
Jones, V. S.	47
Kansas Experiment Station, State Agricultural College, Reports of	83, 100
Kansas Farmer	39, 40
Kansas State Board of Agriculture, Bulletins of	94
Kansas State Board of Agriculture, Reports of	18, 26, 33, 34, 37, 40, 58, 99, 100, 102, 103
Kansas State Horticultural Society, Reports of	59, 69, 70, 75, 77, 80, 82, 84, 91
Kansas State Horticultural Society, Transactions of	73, 77, 80, 81, 84, 86, 88, 92, 102
Kearney county	49
Kellicott, D. S	117
Kelly, D. S.	54

Kerosene emulsion	9
Kiowa county	26
Kitchen, insects in	108
Knapsack sprayers	11
Knaus, Warren	37
Labette county	34, 40
Lady-birds, attacking Chinch-bugs	14
Lady-birds, feeding on Apple-root Louse	74
Lane county	83
Laphygma frugiperda Sm. and Abb.	39
Larva, definition of	3
Laundry, insects in	108
Leavenworth county	34, 40
Le Baron, Wm.	16, 58
Leptocoris trivittatus Say	99
Leucania albilinea Guenée	37
Life-stages of insects, explained	3
Lime	10
Lincoln county	34, 37
Linn county	34
Lintner, J. A.	74, 75, 117
Locusts — see Injurious Grasshoppers, Rocky Mountain Locust.	
Locust tree, insects attacking	103
London purple	8
Long-winged Locust	43
Lygus lineolaris P. Beauv.	80
Lyon county	19, 34, 54
Machines for spraying	11
Maggot, definition of	3
Maple-worm, (see Green-striped Maple-worm)	3, 4
Maple, attacked by Fall Web-worm	84
Maple, insects attacking	84, 99, 101, 103
Marion county	34
Marlatt, C. L.	113
Marlatt, F. H.	113
Marshall county	34
Marten, John	113
Maynard, C. J.	76
McPherson county	34, 37
Melanoplus bivittatus Say	42
Melanoplus differentialis Thomas	42
Melanoplus femur-rubrum De Geer	41
Melanoplus spretus Thomas	22
Melon Beetle — see Cucumber Beetle.	
Melons, insects attacking	65
Metamorphosis, complete, definition of	4
Metamorphosis, incomplete, definition of	5
Miami county	34, 35
Micrococcus insectorum Burrill	15
Millet, attacked by Chinch-bug	13
Mitchell county	34, 83
Montgomery county	34, 77
Morris county	34, 37
Moulting, definition of	5
Murgantia histrionica Hahn	57
Murtfeldt, Mary	54
Mustard, insects attacking	57
Myzus cerasi Fabr.	90
Naphthaline	10

124 INDEX.

Nemaha county	34
Neosho county	34, 77
Newman, M. B.	33
Norton county	34, 83
Nozzle for spraying	11
Orgyia leucostigma Sm. and Abb.	96
Osborn, Herbert	47, 48, 49, 117
Osborne county	34, 37
Osage county	34, 77
Ottawa county	34, 37
Paris green	7
Pea, insects attacking	62
Pea-weevil	4, 62, 63, 64
Peach, insects attacking	91, 103
Peach-tree Borer	91
Pear, insects attacking	69, 80, 103
Periplaneta orientalis Linn.	108
Persian insect powder	9
Phlegethontius carolina Linn	61
Phoxopteris comptana Froel	94
Pieris protodice Boisd.	60
Pieris rapæ Linn.	59
Platygaster sp., parasite of Hessian Fly	31
Plum Curculio	87, 89
Plum Gouger	89
Plum, insects attacking	80, 87, 89, 103
Plusia brassicæ Riley	61
Popenoe, E. A.	18, 21, 26, 58, 62, 64, 80, 81, 83, 92, 100, 113
Pottawatomie county	34
Powder guns	11
Prairie Farmer	16, 28
Prevention	12
Pteromalus sp., parasite on Wheat-straw Worm	37
Pupa, definition of	4
Pyrethrum	9
Quail, as a natural remedy for the Chinch-bug	14
Quince, attacked by Fall Web-worm	84
Quince, insects attacking	69, 80, 103
Railliet	114
Raspberry, insects attacking	93
Raspberry Saw-fly	4, 10
Raspberry Slug	93, 107
Red-legged Locust	22, 11
Red Spider	106
Remedies	6, 7
Reno county	34
Report, First Annual, of the Director of the Experiment Station, University of Kansas,	15
Report of Experiment Station, Kansas State Agricultural College	64, 83, 100
Reports of Kansas State Board of Agriculture	18, 26, 33, 34, 37, 40, 58, 99, 100, 102, 103
Reports of the Kansas State Horticultural Society	59, 69, 70, 75, 77, 80, 82, 84, 91
Report of State Entomologist of Illinois	58
Report of State Entomologist of Missouri	28, 38, 102
Report of U. S. Entomological Commission	31
Rice county	37
Riley county	22, 24, 34, 100, 113
Riley, C. V.	8, 23, 28, 38, 39, 42, 43, 46, 48, 51, 60, 64, 89, 102, 108, 110, 111, 113, 115, 116
Rocky Mountain Locust	22, 42, 44, 45
Rocky Mountain Locust, attacking garden crops	66
Rocky Mountain Locust, attacking grasses and cereals other than corn and wheat	49

INDEX.

Rocky Mountain Locust, attacking large fruits	92
Rocky Mountain Locust, attacking shade-trees	105
Rocky Mountain Locust, attacking small fruits	95
Rocky Mountain Locust, attacking wheat	40
Rolfs, P. H.	117
Rooks county	34
Rose Slug	106
Rose-slug Saw-fly	4, 10
Round-headed Apple-tree Borer	67, 70, 71, 75
Rush county	34, 37, 38
Russell county	34, 37
Saline county	34, 37
Saperda candida Fabr	67
Saunders, Wm	69, 84, 86
Say, Thomas	69
Schizoneura lanigera Hausm	74
Sedgwick county	34, 105
Selandria rosæ Harr	106
Selandria rubi Harris	93
Semiotellus destructor, parasite of Hessian Fly	31
Shade-trees, insects attacking	96, 105
Sharpless, Thomas	116
Shawnee county	34, 52
Sherman county	37
Simmons, L. A.	73
Smith county	34
Smith, J. B.	8, 9, 116
Snow, F. H.	14, 15, 18, 26, 33, 34, 37, 40, 60, 94, 99, 1-2, 103
Southern Cabbage-worm	60
Southern Corn-root Worm	19
Southern Corn-root Worm, attacking garden crops	66
Southern Corn-root Worm, attacking grasses and cereals other than corn and wheat	49
Sporotrichum globuliferum Speg	15
Sprayers — see Knapsack Sprayers.	
Spraying and dusting	10
Spring Canker-worm	3, 7, 75
Squash Bug	2, 5, 7, 56
Squash, insects attacking	56, 65
Stable Fly — see Cattle Fly.	
Stafford county	39
Stored grain, insects attacking	50
Strawberries, injured by Tarnished Plant-bug	81
Strawberries, insects attacking	80, 81, 94
Strawberry Leaf-roller	94
Sucking Insects	1
Sumner county	34
Sweet potatoes, insects attacking	55
Tarnished Plant-bug	80, 95
Tarnished Plant-bug, attacking small fruits	95
Tetranychus telarius Linn	106
Thyridopteryx ephemeræformis Haworth	103
Tinea pellionella Linn	110
Tobacco	10
Tomato, insects attacking	64, 66
Tomato Worm	2, 3, 7, 64
Tortoise Beetles	55
Transactions of Kansas State Horticultural Society	73, 77, 80, 81, 84, 86, 88, 92, 102
Turnip, insects attacking	57
Tussock-moth Worm	3

Two-striped Locust. ... 12
Tyroglyphus sp. ... 53
U. S. Commissioner of Agriculture, Report of ... 16
U. S. Entomological Commission, Report of ... 31
Van Deman, H. E. ... 73
Vegetables, insects attacking ... 66
Wabaunsee county ... 34
Walnut Moth ... 98
Walnut, attacked by Fall Web-worm ... 85
Walnut, insects attacking ... 98
Walnut Moth, attacking large fruits ... 92
Walnut-moth Worm ... 3
Washington county ... 34
Weed, C. F. ... 81
Weed, H. E. ... 117
Weevils — see Grain Weevils.
Western Corn-root Worm ... 17, 19
Wheat, attacked by Chinch-bug ... 13
Wheat-head Army Worm ... 3, 37
Wheat, insects attacking ... 29, 40
Wheat Midge ... 7
Wheat-straw Worm ... 35
White hellebore — see Hellebore.
White-marked Tussock-moth ... 96
White-marked Tussock-moth, attacking the apple ... 92
Williston, S. W. ... 113, 116
Wilson county ... 34, 77
Woodson county ... 34, 77
Woolens, insects attacking ... 116
Wyandotte county ... 33, 34

www.ingramcontent.com/pod-product-compliance
Lightning Source LLC
Chambersburg PA
CBHW020103170426
43199CB00009B/376